American Film and Society Since 1945

The Contemporary United States

Series Editors: CHRISTOPHER BROOKEMAN AND WILLIAM ISSEL

PUBLISHED TITLES

FORTHCOMING TITLES

AMERICAN FILM AND SOCIETY SINCE 1945

Leonard Quart and Albert Auster

MACMILLAN

First published 1984 by
Higher and Further Education Division
MACMILLAN PUBLISHERS LTD
London and Basingstoke
Companies and representatives
throughout the world

An extract from Chapter 4 has been
published in *Cineaste*, 13, No. 2 (February 1984)

Typeset by
Wessex Typesetters Ltd
Frome, Somerset

Printed and bound in Great Britain at
The Camelot Press Ltd, Southampton

British Library Cataloguing in Publication Data
Quart, Leonard
   American film and society since 1945.—(Contemporary United States)
   1.   Moving-pictures—United States—History—Social aspects
   I. Title   II. Auster, Albert   III. Series
   306′.485   PN1993.5.U6
   ISBN 0–333–30021–1
   ISBN 0–333–30023–8 pbk

Contents

List of Plates

1. *The Best Years of Our Lives*: the marriage of Homer (Harold Russell) and Wilma (Cathy O'Donnell) – the reaffirmation of the American Dream.
2. *Singin' in the Rain*: Gene Kelly's exultant dance – the apotheosis of fifties' optimism. From the MGM release 'SINGIN' IN THE RAIN'. © 1952 Loew's Incorporated. Renewed 1979 Metro-Goldwyn-Mayer Inc.
3. *Easy Rider*: Wyatt (Peter Fonda) and Billy (Dennis Hopper) on the road – a film which captures some of the prime themes of the counterculture and the sixties. © Columbia Pictures.
4. *The Godfather II*: a close-up of a sombre, remote Michael Corleone (Al Pacino) – an epic of dissolution, capturing how Americanisation turned a murderous but warm and passionate world into an impersonal, alienated nightmare. © Paramount Pictures Corporation.
5. *Rocky*: white, working-class hero Rocky (Sylvester Stallone) fighting for the heavyweight championship against the black champion Appollo Creed – a seventies' film which affirms traditional American values like the Horatio Alger dream of moving from 'rags to riches'. From the United Artists release 'ROCKY'. © 1977 United Artists Corporation.
6. *On Golden Pond*: Fonda and Hepburn as the aging Thayers – a conjuring up of cinematic memories and Hollywood iconography in the eighties. © MCA Incorporated.

Every effort has been made to trace all copyright holders but if any have been inadvertently overlooked, the publishers will be pleased to make the necessary arrangements at the first opportunity.

Acknowledgements

ALTHOUGH the act of writing is often considered a solitary one, there are always people whose love, support and assistance are invaluable in that lonely and isolated process. Therefore we wish to acknowledge Barbara, Alissa and Luba Quart, and Molly Auster, for their love. And we also wish to acknowledge the editors of *Cineaste* magazine, Gary Crowdus, Dan Georgakas, and Lenny Rubenstein who aided us in critical moments in our writing careers. And especially Chris Brookeman, who as one of the editors of this series made invaluable comments, suggestions and criticisms along the way. In addition, our editors at Macmillan, Sarah Mahaffy and Vanessa Peerless, were patient and responsive. Finally, a note of thanks to Loretta Seidenfaden and Jean Arnold who typed an often difficult to decipher manuscript.

Editors' Preface

MENTION the United States and few people respond with feelings of neutrality. Discussions about the role of the United States in the contemporary world typically evoke a sense of admiration or a shudder of dislike. Pundits and politicians alike make sweeping references to attributes of modern society deemed 'characteristically American'. Yet qualifications are in order, especially regarding the distinctiveness of American society and the uniqueness of American culture. True, American society has been shaped by the size of the country, the migratory habits of the people and the federal system of government. Certainly, American culture cannot be understood apart from its multi-cultural character, its irreverence for tradition and its worship of technological imagery. It is equally true, however, that life in the United States has been profoundly shaped by the dynamics of American capitalism and by the penetration of capitalist market imperatives into all aspects of daily life.

The series is designed to take advantage of the growth of specialised research about post-war America in order to foster understanding of the period as a whole as well as to offer a critical assessment of the leading developments of the post-war years. Coming to terms with the United States since 1945 requires a willingness to accept complexity and ambiguity, for the history encompasses conflict as well as consensus, hope as well as despair, progress as well as stagnation. Each book in the series offers an interpretation designed to spark discussion rather than a definitive account intended to close debate. The series as a whole is meant to offer students, teachers and the general public fresh perspectives and new insights about the contemporary United States.

CHRISTOPHER BROOKEMAN
WILLIAM ISSEL

1. Introduction

'From shadows and symbols into the truth.'
John Henry, Cardinal Newman

In 1981, thirty-five years after it was first produced, John Huston's almost legendary Second World War documentary about psychologically crippled veterans, *Let There Be Light* (1945), received its first commercial public showing. Originally suppressed by the US Defense Department, which feared its possible pacifistic influence, interest in it and its reputation were kept alive by film critics (most notably James Agee, who even included it on his best films list of 1946). Unfortunately time had not dealt too well with *Let There Be Light*, and most contemporary film critics found it ingenuous and naive to the point of simplemindedness.[1]

Nevertheless, despite the fact that *Let There Be Light* failed to live up to its critical reputation, it still succeeded on another quite unforeseen level. As a matter of fact the showing of the film might be compared to lifting the lid on a time capsule – one that revealed not only an era's artifacts but conveyed a sense of its cultural and social moods as well. Indeed, one critic indirectly put his finger on this when he criticised the film for being 'unduly optimistic'.[2] And undoubtedly by contemporary standards any film that communicates *Let There Be Light*'s magical faith in the healing power of psychiatrists and Freudianism clearly displays a degree of complacency that could hardly be emulated by today's more pessimistic films. Therefore, although *Let There Be Light* may have failed thoroughly to impress modern critics with its moving portrayal of the plight of shell-shocked soldiers, it did nonetheless indirectly provide a powerful insight into the political and intellectual assumptions of the post-war era.

It is hardly an original point – though one that bears repeating – that films have the ability to evoke the authentic tone of a society and a particular era. However, there was a time when a number of historians and social scientists were hesitant about accepting this truism. By films one does not mean merely documentaries, which obviously directly convey something of the reality of the way people live and feel, but also commercial, fiction films. It is not only that films sometimes evoke and imitate the surfaces of day-to-day life, the way people talk, dress, consume (though social realism is clearly not one of Hollywood's prime commitments); but more significantly and problematically, fictional films reveal something of the dreams, desires, displacements and even the issues confronting American society.

Clearly films are a powerful and significant form. As art historian and critic Erwin Panofsky has suggested, their absence from our lives would probably constitute a 'social catastrophe'.[3] He wrote: 'If all the serious lyric poets, composers, painters and sculptors were forced by law to stop their activities, a rather small fraction of the general public would seriously regret it. If the same thing were to happen with the movies the social consequences would be catastrophic.'[4] That is probably an overstatement, but films shown in theatres, on television and video cassettes are clearly some of the prime forms of entertainment for the general public and one of the most democratic elements in the cultural fabric.

Their being important to the public does not necessarily mean that they are a significant form of cultural and historical evidence. But the fact that they reach large numbers of people must signify that films do connect with some aspect of the experience (conscious or unconscious) of the general public or at least a large subculture contained within it. Of course it is absurd to claim that the writers, directors and producers of films (be they assembly line products or works expressing an individual sensibility) have some mystical intuition into the *zeitgeist*. Nevertheless, the makers of films are touched by the same tensions and fantasies as everyone else, and their profits are usually dependent on their ability to guess or divine popular feelings and trends. So though no straight line can be drawn between the film industry and the popular mind, neither is it a mirror of public feelings and habits, nor can one make the vulgar, mechanistic connection which implies that the industry determines the social values and political opinions of a supine public. However, there is no question that films can both reflect and reinforce popular preconceptions, and for some Americans cinematic images (given their directness and immediacy) can sadly become a substitute for reality itself.

In America in the last few years a number of historians and culture critics have begun to give films their due as important social and cultural evidence. Especially noteworthy is the work of John O'Connor and Martin Jackson (*American History/American Film*), Robert Sklar (*Movie Made America*), Andrew Bergman (*We're In The Money*), and Garth Jowett (*Film: The Democratic Art*). In fact, so far may the pendulum have swung that for a number of historians films have come to be one of the most important clues to understanding the state of the American mind. As Arthur Schlesinger Jr has said, albeit in an inflated manner:

> Strike the American contribution from drama, painting, music, sculpture and even dance, and possibly poetry and the novel and the world's achievement is only marginally diminished. But the film without American contribution is unimaginable. The fact that film has been the most potent vehicle for the American imagination suggests all the more strongly that movies have something to tell us not just about the surfaces but the mysteries of American life.[5]

Of course, stating this is much easier than defining precisely how we can penetrate those surfaces and reveal those mysteries. For one thing, as we noted previously, it is always dangerous and simplistic to assume any direct link between film and popular thought. American films have been and are still often bound by genre conventions, censorship, and the star system; and their major thrust has rarely been consciously to illuminate the culture and society, but to mythologise and evade — simultaneously to provide glamour, escape and security. (Despite the appearance at times of subversive and disruptive elements, American films usually conclude by supporting the rightness of the dominant social value system.) And the trends and tendencies within the popular mind are as varied as the audience itself – divided by age, social class, region, ethnicity, race, etc., and often fickle and changeable in its response. Thus, the effort to explore and define how films project the basic assumptions, moods and problems of a society must be by its very nature tentative, ambiguous and problematic. However, in the act of either trivialising, repressing or stylising social and psychological reality, Hollywood was able to create resonant and suggestive images, characters, dialogue and behaviour that both reflected and helped shape the audience's consciousness, granting us much insight into American culture. This evidence, often so difficult to decipher, for Hollywood's vision was more often implicit than direct and explicit (few Hollywood directors had an articulate, coherent or systematic political or social perspective), is as important to analyse as histories of the industry, the nature of directorial sensibility, or the diverse genre forms produced by Hollywood.

That is not to say that auterist critics, who promoted the notion that the basic starting point of film is the personal sensibility, style or motifs of the director, did not make some contribution to understanding the connection between American film and culture. Though clearly more interested in defending (even glorifying) the aesthetic value of the Hollywood studio films than in exploring their social meaning, auterist critics like Andrew Sarris (writing in *Film Culture* & *Village Voice*) did capture how John Ford's vision of family and community has permeated and remained constant through such diverse films as *The Grapes of Wrath* (1940) and *She Wore a Yellow Ribbon* (1949). However, auteur critics were, in their unsystematic, polemical and sometimes shrill manner, primarily interested in demonstrating how a film's visual style and directorial signature were more significant than its subject matter (for example, a Budd Boetticher western being of much greater aesthetic value than a Stanley Kramer or Richard Brooks social-problem film), and consequently were able to redeem and sometimes create the critical reputations of directors such as Howard Hawks, Nicholas Ray, Douglas Sirk and other less deserving figures.

In doing that the auteur critics granted added lustre and cultural importance to Hollywood genres like the thriller, screwball comedy and the woman's picture. Of course these genres themselves were subject to a body of criticism which explored their themes, structures and iconography. Genre criticism often traced the shifts in the form's conventions and themes (for example, the changes in the western from Tom Mix through John Ford to Sam Peckinpah) or examined the relation of the genre to its audience. Most genre critics were more interested in analysing the films as self-contained forms, dissecting the iconography of the musical rather than evoking its cultural and social significance. However, other critics such as Robert Warshow and Leo Braudy sought to analyse the relationship between a genre's popularity and the attitudes and needs that audiences bring to it.

There have also been film critics who have directly sought to unravel the ambiguous psychological and social nature of the film. For instance, the landmark work of Siegfried Kracauer, *From Caligari to Hitler*, although marred by too heady a faith in these films' ability to reveal the secrets of the collective mind as well as predict the rise of Nazism, still yields interesting insight into film as a means of illuminating the 'deepest psychological dispositions'[6] of a society. This, coupled with the Freudian notion that films, like dreams, have a latent and manifest content, has proved of value in wringing social meaning from even the most escapist of films.

Nonetheless, these perceptions are weakened by the fact that they make the meaning of a film dependent on some kind of unconscious activity. It is impossible to demonstrate how the Jungian 'collective unconscious' (even if we accept its existence) or the latent content of Freudianism manifests itself in the narrative and imagery of the film. A critic must maintain an almost mystical faith that it does, or more commonly merely see it as speculation and feel it unnecessary to prove its existence. But in writing about notions such as the mass unconscious, there is a tendency to project elaborate meanings on to the most commonplace of films. As a result, the work of art becomes something secondary, even insignificant; what becomes all-important is the analysis and interpretation, or else, as in the words of Paddy Whannel and Stuart Hall, art (film in this case) becomes merely 'sugar on the pill'.[7]

In contrast, there is the more synthetic, humanistic idea posed by Raymond Williams and others about art – which can also be applied to film – that art is a means to 'learn, describe, to understand, to educate';[8] that it is not only a source of unconscious feelings, but has a variety of political, cultural and aesthetic meanings and functions. In writing this book we set out, influenced by genre, auteur, psychoanalytic, Marxist and other critical perspectives (but not wedded to any one of them) to observe and evaluate, both politically and aesthetically, how American film conveys its social and cultural values and commitments, and even what solutions it sometimes offers for society's problems. Given our belief in film's historical and social significance, it is the particular purpose of this study to look at American films from 1945 to the present and analyse how they perceived and conjured up the American social and cultural landscape.

To accomplish this our method is a simple one. For one thing, since almost 95 per cent of the film time on the American screens (and a large percentage on foreign ones as well) is dominated by Hollywood films, we have treated Hollywood and American film as being synonymous. (We have left out avant-garde and most documentary films from our study.) Similarly, although we are aware of the hazards of adopting a decade-by-decade approach (clearly the sixties did not end on 31 December 1969, and the Cold War and the anti-communist crusade were not limited to one decade) it nevertheless has the advantage of convenience and popular acceptance (references to the 'fifties and sixties' denote a particular set of values and assumptions). In addition, this decade-by-decade approach has allowed us to include in capsule form some of the major events and ideas that dominated a decade and left their mark on its films.

Needless to say, a serious difficulty was the selection of films that best illuminated these trends. In order to accomplish this we have relied in the main on a large body of films that could be called 'public classics'[9] – films whose box office grosses, awards and critical reputation (which have either stood the test of time or grown with it) indicate by their broad acceptance that they have a connection with public consciousness. Undoubtedly, there are many other films that might point in different directions, deal with the themes we have delineated in a clearer, sharper manner, or were perhaps visionary in their ability to herald future trends and themes. Nevertheless, it does seem to us that some degree of consensus exists about the importance of specific films and their relation to the society of their times (for example, *The Best Years of Our Lives* and the forties, *Rebel Without a Cause* and the fifties, *Bonnie and Clyde* and *Easy Rider* and the sixties). It is these we have included in our study. Also, although this was by no means the decisive factor in our choice, since this book was intended as both an introduction and a guide to American film and culture for students, we have tried to include films that are accessible to them through rental services and available archives.

Finally, as far as the theme of this study goes, it is important to return for a moment to *Let There Be Light*. When that film is placed alongside some films of the sixties and seventies dealing with similar problems and themes (such as *M*A*S*H*, 1970, *The Deerhunter*, 1978, *Coming Home*, 1978, and a documentary like *Hearts and Minds*, 1974) one cannot escape concluding what a different image they present of America and how that image has changed. For example, in *Let There Be Light* the officer informs (without irony) the just-discharged patients that: 'On your shoulders falls much of the responsibility for the post-war world'. It is an uplifting sentiment that the irreverent surgeons of *M*A*S*H* would dismiss with a contemptuous wisecrack, and the traumatised Vietnam war veterans, Nicky (*The Deerhunter*) and Bob (*Coming Home*), would greet with the stony stare of suicidal despair. In essence our study follows this sort of course, and throughout the book we have attempted to show how American films from the late forties (Hollywood at its zenith) moved from a relatively self-confident affirmation of the American Dream to the films of the sixties and seventies, where despite the continued emphasis on big budgets, stars and genre formulae the films grew increasingly more anxious, alienated and nihilistic. In constructing this pattern we have tried to avoid simplifying the complex and contradictory history of these films. We have been conscious of the feelings of doubt and loss that began to appear beneath the buoyant surface of forties' films, and the preservation of American dream imagery in the darker, more pessimistic work of the sixties and seventies.

Ultimately, what we have written is only one more step in the ongoing and complex study of the manifold and diverse interactions of culture and society, and more specifically film and society. We have not conceived this book as a definitive work, but as one that is part of the process whose aim is to use film as one means to gain a sense of the American ethos. For we believe, as did James Agee on writing his first film review in *The Nation*, that the final function of any review or critical study is to aid those who 'watch any given screen, where the proof is caught irrelevant to excuse, and available in proportion to the eye which sees it, and the mind which uses it'.[10]

2. The Forties

In 1936 President Franklin D. Roosevelt announced that Americans had a 'rendezvous with destiny'. It was the war years that turned that prophecy into a reality as America emerged from its traditional isolationism and became the most powerful country in the world – an imperialist, interventionist nation. Indeed, the energy that had once gone into the struggle against the Depression was now concentrated on the war effort. And that effort granted to many people on the home-front a sense of purpose, exhilaration and community that was rare in American history.[1]

The same energy and optimism that helped bring about victory carried over into the post-war years. However, this optimism had more to do with people's material well-being (in the 1940s the average American enjoyed an income fifteen times greater than the average foreigner)[2] and national pride than with any new political and social commitments. In fact, most Americans were weary with the Depression and foreign wars, and bored with politics. Bursting with the enforced savings of the Second World War Americans wanted to enjoy their new-found prosperity and victory. A new era seemed about to open for them, offering not only increased income to ordinary Americans, but a chance for education and greater status.

A driving force behind this new climate was the GI Bill of Rights which became law in 1944, helping returning veterans to borrow money to set up businesses, and attend universities which they had once perceived as preserves of the upper middle class. Furthermore, a baby boom provided evidence that Americans felt released from the anguish of the past decade and a half, and had a sense of infinite promise in the future.[3]

Another key factor in this changing climate was the accession to the presidency of Vice President Harry S. Truman, upon the death of F. D. R. in 1945. A moderate, party organisation stalwart from Missouri, Truman at first suffered by comparison with the charismatic Roosevelt. In addition, he was beset by a resurgent conservative congressional coalition of Southern Democrats (Dixiecrats) and Republicans, who frustrated his attempts to extend the New Deal, and forced him to watch helplessly as they overrode his veto of the anti-labour Taft–Hartley bill. However, even after he came into his own after a startling come-from-behind victory in the presidential campaign of 1948, it was only to introduce a Fair Deal programme that was merely a pale copy and codification of the New Deal. Thus, despite his triumph, the profits and prestige of the Truman era were owned by the corporations rather than by the forces of social reform.[4]

Nevertheless, although abundance and a sense of the irrelevance of social conflict were the themes of the forties there were storm clouds on the horizon. A crippling strike wave, culminating in a coal strike led by F. D. R.'s nemesis John L. Lewis, served notice that labour was no longer willing to continue its rather unequal collaboration with business and wanted a larger share of the wealth generated by the war. This labour insurgency coupled with high inflation caused ripples of anxiety on the economic landscape. Equally significant, though largely beneath the surface, were a pair of demographic changes. One of these was the great migration of poor blacks to the North to work in defence plants where they exchanged the certainties and oppression of rural life for the anxieties and higher wages of the cities. Simultaneous with this black migration was the movement of whites (aided by low-interest Federal Housing Administration and Veterans' Administration loans) to the suburbs. Hand in hand, the twin migrations would alter the social fabric of America.[5]

However severe these labour problems and demographic changes were they were merely minor irritants compared to the upsets caused by foreign affairs. Long used to neglecting foreign relationships, the Americans were thrust by the war into a leading international position. It also pushed them into an alliance with the Soviet Union – a nation considered in some pre-war American circles as a greater menace than Germany,

Italy or Japan. Nonetheless, most Americans were little disturbed by the wartime alliance with Russia. In fact, many liberals saw that alliance (with Russia as the junior partner) as the basis of an enduring peace wherein post-war social reforms would become the prime commitment of both nations. Yet among conservatives there were always undercurrents of suspicion of Russia and towards the US–Soviet Alliance. And when Stalin in quest of greater security broke the Yalta agreements, conservative unease and anger toward Russia increased, a wariness which many liberals soon began to share.[6]

Indeed during the next few years, despite the dream of a new international order embodied in the UN, the Cold War, as it came to be known, escalated, and relations between the US and the Soviet Union became permeated with fear, suspicion and distrust. As a result the two ideologically expansionist powers, their wartime co-operation seemingly forgotten, now confronted each other without either side genuinely seeking peace or rapprochement. On their side the Americans continually evoked images of an 'iron curtain' and the threat of Soviet expansion, while the Russians talked of 'American imperialism' and the constant threat to their borders and security.[7]

Needless to say the conflict was not solely confined to rhetoric. In 1947, breaking with a long-standing American tradition against peacetime military and political alliances, President Truman gained congressional approval for 400 million dollars in military and economic aid to Greece and Turkey to help them in their struggle against communist guerrillas. This action, soon to be dubbed the Truman doctrine, had broader implications (including the seeds for later American interventions) for in the words of Truman, America was now committed 'to support free people who are resisting attempted subjugation by armed minorities or by outside pressure'.[8]

Swiftly the crisis between the two former allies deepened as a Soviet-sponsored coup in Czechoslovakia eliminated the last vestiges of democracy in eastern and central Europe and the Marshall Plan and the North Atlantic Treaty Organisation established an American-backed *cordon sanitaire* in western Europe. The former American action worked out by diplomat-scholar George F. Kennan and his State Department policy planning group and politically sponsored by Secretary of State George C. Marshall reasoned that anti-communism was not enough to impede the spread of communism in Europe. They held that it was only with the recovery of the European economy (one that would also provide markets for the US) that the Soviet threat could be thwarted. Indeed with the passage of the Marshall Plan in 1948 western Europe did take a giant step towards economic recovery and enhanced its ability to resist communism.[9]

However, even with western Europe stabilised by 1949, American anxieties about communism hardly lessened. In fact the fear of communist aggression from abroad was soon replaced by terror over a native communist fifth column whose simultaneous task it seemed to be to ferret out American military secrets as they subverted their will to resist. A seemingly continuous series of spy ring revelations (Igor Gouzenko, Judith Coplon, Elizabeth Bentley and Whittaker Chambers) reinforced these feelings, and the explosion of a Soviet A-bomb coupled with the fall of mainland China to the communists fanned them into a full-fledged anti-communist hysteria. Angered by this growing communist menace and now anxious over their own survival, Americans sought easy answers and quick solutions. Thus, rather than confront the long-term and powerful economic and social causes that produced communism, Americans found the reasons for its success in an international communist conspiracy.[10]

In the vanguard of this search for traitors was the House Un-American Activities Committee (HUAC). Dormant during the war years, the committee saw its chance to regain the limelight in 1947 when it held hearings investigating communist influence in the motion picture industry. Drawn by the prestige and glamour of the film industry, the committee was more interested in the political affiliations of its ten 'unfriendly' witnesses – some of whom were the most talented and politically active writers and directors in Hollywood (for example Dalton Trumbo, Albert Maltz, Ring Lardner Jr) – than in the supposedly subversive content of their films.[11]

At first the moguls and liberals in the industry protested about the committee's actions, but seeing the 'ten' take the first amendment in regard to their politics they quickly succumbed to expediency, fearing their profits and careers might be threatened. As a result, in a meeting at the Waldorf-Astoria hotel soon after the 'ten' appeared before the committee they issued their craven 'Waldorf Statement' which was in essence a tacit agreement to establish a blacklist refusing to re-employ the 'Hollywood Ten' or other members of the Communist Party.[12]

Of course the HUAC investigations of Hollywood were just one element of the growing fear of and attack on the presumed communist conspiracy. In 1949 the leaders of the US Communist Party were convicted under the Smith Act for conspiracy and sent to prison. More significantly, the deeply symbolic Hiss–Chambers affair, which saw the former high level New Deal bureaucrat Alger Hiss accused of espionage and convicted of perjury, brought the New Deal under attack for being soft on communism. In fact the forties concluded with a portion of the public (for example mid-westerners, recent immigrants, and Catholics) holding that New Deal liberalism and communism were one and the same thing.[13]

All the same, despite the growing fear of the 'red menace' the forties were still essentially a time of optimism and consensus, and nowhere was this more evident than in the American film. In fact, although they had their dark side, touched with pessimism and self-doubt, the movies basically endorsed and nurtured the American dream at the same time as they reflected a feeling of national triumph. Moreover, for the industry itself the post-war era was a boom time. As a matter of fact from 1942–44 Hollywood produced about 440 films a year, and 1946 was the most commercially successful year in its history. The forties were a time of big stars and big audiences where the studios with their armies of talent and technicians reigned supreme. And though the last few years of the decade saw Hollywood beset by labour troubles, adverse Supreme Court decisions (the Paramount case), and the after-effects of the HUAC hearings (the blacklisting of a large number of major creative contributors to the industry), the forties can still be seen as 'the last great show of confidence and skill' by Hollywood before it became paralysed by the competition from television and the death of the studio system.[14]

Nowhere was this optimism more evident than in the war films that the studios churned out through the war years. The overriding purpose of these films was patriotic uplift, and despite the fact that an occasional hero lapsed into *Casablanca* (1942)-like cynicism or malaise, they were eventually aroused to a consciousness of the need for collective struggle against fascism. With Hollywood thus shouldering the wartime burden of maintaining morale, there were few films that dealt with the reality rather than the romance of combat, or with the psychological effects of the war. Those that did, such as John Huston's pacifistic documentary, *Battle of San Pietro* (1945), which with great immediacy and intensity conveyed haunting and harrowing images of the war, were prevented by the Pentagon from reaching the public. The Pentagon and Hollywood did not want films which filled the screens with images of crying children, cemeteries of dog tags and exhausted terrified peasants. What they did want were war films which exhorted Americanness, creating mythical, ethnically and occupationally heterogeneous platoons which were supposed to be the embodiment of American democracy.

However, by the end of the war, with victory clearly in sight, self-righteous propagandistic films like *The Purple Heart* (1944) and *God is My Co-Pilot* (1943) gave way to films that were more sophisticated and realistic. Among the first of these was Lewis Milestones' *A Walk in the Sun* (1945), which though it was able to convey a realistic sense of fear and anxiety among its melting pot infantry unit through its subtle use of close ups, darkness, light and shadow, still contained a multi-ethnic cast of characters devoid of complexity and nuance. Its characters tended at times to undermine the reality of the film with self-conscious, literary interior monologues and tiresome banter. The film also provides a sentimental image of the 'dogfaces' that personified American democracy. And though the film does succeed in subordinating stars like Dana Andrews to the courage of the collective, the pseudo-democratic (Popular Front) clichés and rhetoric about the 'mighty good Joes' and their folksy wisdom can become cloying. Yet in the power of its images and its relatively non-heroic, unromantic treatment of the war, *A Walk in the Sun* was head and shoulders above the run of the mill war films with their bloodthirsty and barbaric 'Nips' and 'Krauts' being put to rout by the derring-do of Errol Flynn and John Wayne.

Similarly, William Wellman's *The Story of G.I. Joe* (1945) combined both the documentary and the fictional in a way that gave real meaning to the sacrifices and pain of war. In fact there are moments in this story of one exhausted platoon's experiences at the battle of San Pietro that are almost too powerful to bear. Such is the case with the breakdown of tough sergeant Freddie Steele, and the death of the captain of the platoon, Robert Mitchum, whose quiet dignity and strength turned him into a towering, almost tragic figure. These were elements that moved critic James Agee to compare the film, especially its final moments, to a Whitmanesque war poem.[15]

In a far different mode was John Ford's romantic and leisurely *They Were Expendable* (1945), which was a work of myth rather than history. Ford's film displayed little interest in the pyschology or sociology of his PT boat officers and crew, but was passionately committed to paying homage to the community of men who were gallant and heroic in defeat. The film was filled with epic long shots of beautifully composed, almost painterly sea battles, and of the ritual of sailors' arrivals and departures into battle. Ford of course believed in the virtues of the military: he conceived of it as a community built on a hierarchic code of power, self-sacrifice, responsibility and obligation. The film's officers are heroes, men devoid of fear and, in the case of John Wayne, unwilling to allow mere wounds to prevent them from going into battle. But they also understand that leadership demands that they subordinate individual desires for the good of the squadron – to become 'team players'.

Ford's film was a celebration, not a critical analysis of the American war effort. *They Were Expendable* is filled with patriotic sentiments – a sound track playing 'The Battle Hymn of the Republic' and 'Red River Valley', a montage of wounded men – one of them who is blind smoking a cigarette with trembling hands – and a full shot of exhausted courageous nurses walking in silhouette through a hospital corridor. Thus it should come as no surprise, with such homage to the military, that the film's

apotheosis is the appearance of Ford's deity, General Mac-
Arthur, accompanied by a series of reaction shots of sailors
with glowing faces standing in awe of this American icon.

In the hands of another director without the pictorial or
narrative gifts of Ford these rituals and stereotypes might have
descended to mere historical tableaux. However, such is Ford's
honest feeling for the rituals and codes, and the images are so
grand and stately that the conventional and sentimental
emotions and characters are transformed into archetypes, and
the clichés into myths.

No less important in raising morale and maintaining commitment to the war effort than some of the flag-waving combat
films were the home-front melodramas. In fact, a film such as
David O. Selznick's *Since You Went Away* (1944) actually opened
with the announcement: 'This is the story of an unconquerable
fortress, the American home, 1943'. What followed was a
demonstration of the depth of America's and of its womens'
commitment to the war effort. One which even had Claudette
Colbert as its typical suburban housewife leaving her comfortable home for a job in a welding factory where she worked
beside a host of immigrant women who equated her with their
dream of America. In addition, Ms Colbert is the mother and
wife of the All-American Miltons (played by Shirley Temple
and Jennifer Jones), an idealised suburban family who live in a
sparkling clean, soulless world. An innocent virginal milieu,
where an eternally rejected, urbane suitor (Joseph Cotton)
constantly comes back for more from Claudette. Finally, to
make the dream complete there is a black mammy cook (Hattie
McDaniel) who, though the Miltons can no longer afford her,
returns at night, after a full day's work, to provide free
housework, comedy and consolation. An image of racial unity
that provides a filling capstone to this relentless celebration of
home-front USA.

Nevertheless, despite its wish fulfilment qualities, *Since You
Went Away* did touch on one very important home-front reality,
the new role for women as workers in defence industries – over
four million in 1943 – with many more working in other
industries. A fact which magazines responded to by creating
the symbol of 'Rosie the Riveter', and which Hollywood
reacted to by putting its female stars to work (for example,

Lucille Ball as a defence plant worker in *Meet the People*, 1944). Although this was hardly a great sacrifice it was all the same symbolic of the fact that in a sense everything shot in Hollywood during the years 1942–45, be it combat films such as Walsh's *Objective Burma* (1945), the Tarzan series or Donald Duck cartoons, reflected or was actively committed to the war effort.

However, as the war came to a close, Hollywood began to turn from making films about the war to those that would help ease the transition from war to peace. Here it was the symbol of the returned veteran who became the embodiment of those issues. As a matter of fact, as Dr Franklin Fearing wrote in the first issue of the *Hollywood Quarterly* (predecessor of the present *Film Quarterly*):

'When Johnny Comes Marching Home' is not only the title of a popular Civil War song, it is a symbol and a situation. It is a symbol with curiously ambivalent meanings, it signifies the return of heroes, or wars ended, of happy reunions after hardwon but glorious victories, and of peace after battle. It is also a sign of dissension, of nervous uncertainty lest, in truth, we have not prepared a 'land fit for heroes,' of anxiety regarding possible capacity to adjust and even curiously of fear and hostility. The laughter and tears which welcome Johnny home reflect honest joy and relief, but there is an undertone of nervous tension. Has he changed? How much have I changed? Can we get along together? What is ahead?[16]

It was this kind of anxiety that a film such as *Pride of the Marines* (1945) was intended to assuage. The film itself was taken from the real life experiences of marine hero Al Schmid (John Garfield), who was blinded at Guadalcanal. After detailing Al's early life and his wounding, the film also presents his subsequent withdrawal into a shell of rage and resentment. In the hospital ward other veterans with problems like Al's overcome them by believing that the country will take care of them with the GI Bill, or that just standing up for your rights will get you heard. However, Al remains unconvinced that there is a place for him in civilian society and the film makes it clear that the problem is Al's, not America's. With the issue thus rendered psychological and the society absolved, the usual Hollywood solution is easily wrought. His fiancée confronts his self-pity and tells Al she needs him and naturally his neurosis (as does our concern about the fate of the returned veteran) dissolves.

The same theme of post-war adjustment was taken up by *Till the End of Time* (1946) where the crippled veteran has no girlfriend, but a mother and a friendly army officer who rouse him from his anger and withdrawal to enter the world again. But these films paled by comparison with Samuel Goldwyn and William Wyler's *The Best Years of Our Lives* (1946), which dealt with the return home of three Second World War veterans from different social backgrounds, and the psychological, economic and physical problems of readjustment that they confronted.

The Best Years of Our Lives was hailed as a masterpiece when it opened, and even those who criticised it acknowledged its significance. James Agee, for one, wrote that it was 'one of the very few American studio made movies in years that seem to me profoundly pleasing, moving and encouraging'.[17] Similarly, the Marxist and soon to be blacklisted writer-director Abraham Polonsky wrote that 'the area of human character which *The Best Years* makes available to its audience is a landmark in the fog of escapism, meretricious violence and the gimmick plot attitude of the usual movie'.[18]

Praise like this catapulted the film into the realm of an instant classic. And though that judgement was an inflated one – for the film was at times sentimental, intellectually safe and politically simplistic – *The Best Years* still contained more truth and insight about the readjustment of veterans to peacetime than any other forties' film. Moreover, its brilliant and eloquent use of depth of focus, flowing camera movements, and moving reaction shots that focused on the emotions of the characters, made it an unself-consciously beautiful and lyrical film as well.

Needless to say, for all its human qualities, characters and attempts to deal with the problem of readjustment and conversion in post-war American society *The Best Years* was still a carefully balanced and subtly manipulated tribute to the American way of life – to institutions such as the small town, liberal corporate capitalism, the family, and to Hollywood's belief in the redemptive power of love.

Perhaps most glaring of all is the way the film tended to avoid or obfuscate social issues – to dismiss class as a factor in American society – where army comradeship would unself-consciously bring bank officers together with soda jerks. It also personalised political questions such as the problems of GI's who had no capital, desiring to own a business or some land. The answer the film offers, of course, had nothing to do with the changing nature of capitalism or the banking system. The film's liberal banker Al Stephenson (Frederic March) grants small loans in Capra style (for example, *American Madness*), without collateral to any veterans who are respectable and hard-working. In addition, in the best Capra mode, *The Best Years* turns politics into morality, informing its audience that a good-natured, personally egalitarian, 'regular guy' (Al tells a nervous applicant for a loan, 'Don't sir me – I'm just a sergeant') banker can make the system work. The unstated politics inherent in the film is a commitment to creating an America where every man can be a small capitalist.

A consequence of this failure to confront the political realities of the returning veterans' problems allows the film ultimately to define them as purely personal rather than social. For instance, Al comes home to the warm embrace of a supportive wife, Millie (Myrna Loy), and two almost grown children with lives of their own. However, he is uneasy, insecure and sexually tense – drinking and bantering compulsively – feeling some-what alienated from family and job. Al's behaviour suggests more complex feelings (ones that probably existed before the war) about job, family, marriage and self, than the film is willing to pursue. Nonetheless, by the film's conclusion, we are sure that though Al may still drink too much he has begun to feel at ease amidst the domestic warmth and love of family life.

In fact, as in other veterans' films, the family and a woman's love help not only Al but both Fred and Homer to adjust to civilian life. Fred Derry returns home a war hero with ribbons, citations and nightmares from living so close to death. He also comes home without any qualifications for a decent job, except for the one he left and feels degraded by as a soda jerk. Fred is intelligent, cynical, tough and filled with middle-class ambitions, but married to a sexy blonde (Virginia Mayo) who is that particular symbol of anxiety that bedevilled so many GI's – the unfaithful wife. Too narcissistic and independent, Marie cannot offer Fred any support. However, a good women's love does ultimately help rescue Fred, as Al's pert, lively, strong and sensitive daughter Peggy (Theresa Wright) offers him understanding and a shoulder to lean on.

Although Fred's rescue by Peggy and the offer of a job recycling old bombers into pre-fab housing is rather contrived, this subplot provides us with one of the best reasons why *The Best Years* has been assigned a niche in the pantheon of American films. For in its chronicling of Fred's story *The Best Years* offers us one of its formally most dazzling and powerful scenes. A scene which has Fred walking into an aeroplane graveyard overrun with weeds, and containing row upon row of bombers that are going to be turned into scrap (a metaphor for the obsolete Fred), and has him climb into one of the cobwebbed planes. Camera movement, sound and cutting then work to reconstruct the sensation of take-off and flight; there is a close up of a sweating feverish Fred, the sound of engines on the sound track, and the nightmarish shot of Fred through the blurring glass of the cockpit. A sequence which provides us with a profound insight into Fred's relationship to a war that gave him both a sense of power and great pain. And thus by reliving it he gets a chance to exorcise it.

No less moving is the post-war adjustment of the character of Homer (Harold Russell), whose story is also handled with great honesty and reality. Of course its truth is heightened by the fact that Homer is played by a real amputee (an example of the care and reverence that Wyler took in casting the film), who exudes naturalness. In addition, Homer's problem is not his handicap – he has already achieved a great deal of good-humoured self-sufficiency, using his hooks – but the fear that his passive, fragile fiancée, Wilma (Cathy O'Donnell) will reject him. Homer does not want to be pitied or treated as a freak; he rejects Wilma and is forlorn and angry (he rages against his little sister and her friends treating him as a freak), and what he needs is a willingness to accept Wilma's love. However, before the predictable conclusion is reached there are tender understated scenes where Homer's father undresses him and takes off his hooks; and Homer sitting sombrely in the shadows puts Wilma to the test by removing his hooks and describing how helpless he is: Wilma of course passes the test.

Clearly, despite its intellectual limitations *The Best Years'* deeply etched and moving sequences, its formal luminosity, and its memorable characters did provide a genuine glimpse of the post-war American world. Furthermore, though it ultimately allowed each of its characters a graceful re-entry into post-war American society, it nonetheless suggested the painful problems inherent in that return as well as hints that beneath the official optimism there existed feelings of scepticism and doubt.

Nor was this anxiety merely confined to the returned veteran, it also extended to other areas of American life. In fact so pervasive was it that traces of it could even be found in the work of that apostle of Hollywood optimism, Frank Capra. In Capra's very first post-war film, *It's a Wonderful Life* (1946), he began to modify his normal optimism and belief in the 'little people' with a nightmare vision. In the film his mythic, tranquil, small town, Bedford Falls, is destroyed by selfish materialism and turned into a raw, industrial, neon-lit Pottersville (a hellish fantasy possibly inspired by the squalid boom towns that grew up across America in the wake of the wartime industrial boom). Here even his archetypical common man George Bailey (James Stewart) is beset with self-doubt and feelings of resentment. Nevertheless, Capracorn and the spirit of Christmas eventually do triumph, everybody ultimately singing 'Auld Lang Syne' and the significance of each man's life, no matter how ordinary, reaffirmed. However, this time it is a bit more difficult, and Capra must contrive the *deus ex machina* of a cute folksy angel, Clarence (Henry Travers), to bring this film to its benign and joyous climax.

It's a Wonderful Life (1946) was Frank Capra's favourite film and probably his most personal.[19] Its hero George Bailey is the most individualised and psychologically interesting of Capra's visions of the heroic everyman. George is decent, intelligent, caring and doomed to living a life he finds constricting, devoid of adventure, freedom or great success. In fact George, despite the good he does in town (he builds a subdivision of clean, inexpensive new homes) – he is the ultimate good neighbour – feels himself without real identity, a failure.

Unlike some of his earlier films, especially his famous populist trilogy (*Deeds, Mr. Smith* and *Meet John Doe*) this film is more meditative, less dependent on montage and more on long close ups of George Bailey isolated within a frame. Previously, Capra had questioned the validity of his populist politics in *Meet John Doe* (1941), and there were moments of anguish in his other films, but in *It's a Wonderful Life*, the anguish becomes more personal. And it is in the style of forties' films: the doubts expressed dealt more with the nature of identity and self than with society. As a result there is no steely-eyed Edward Arnold to play a corrupt political boss, nor an ominous fascist tycoon to present a threat both to Bailey and to Capra's ethics and politics in the film. Instead there is only Lionel Barrymore playing Potter – the 'meanest man in town' – a solitary Scrooge-like figure who owns slum tenements. Potter is a cartoon, a small-town tyrant who cannot really be taken too seriously. Thus George Bailey's values and social vision cannot really be threatened as were Jefferson Smith's by the public world (that is, the US Senate). George's nightmare (though supposedly elicited by Potter's villainy) comes from within, and is built on rage intense enough for him to cry out to his almost cloyingly sweet wife Mary (Donna Reed), 'Why do we need all these kids!' Although George's anger is finally defused it takes all the Capracorn and sentimentality that Capra can muster to do it. Moreover, there is still the trace of anguish (the true nature of it never made clear) here that all of Capra's genius for manipulating an audience's more sanguine feelings can never quite erase.

What is more, Capra's nightmare sequence, filled as it was with flashing neon lights and a dark shadowy ambience, contained all the elements that were to characterise a whole genre of forties' films. Indeed many of Hollywood's films, especially those dealing with contemporary American life, conveyed a feeling through their sombre black and white photography of claustrophobia and entrapment. Obviously some of the dark oppressive tone derived from the budgetry limits placed on wartime film-making, where lighting had to be cut down and sets substituted for location shooting. Nevertheless, the eerie menace inherent in the films' look was more than an adjustment to industry economics. It was a conscious choice made by the films' directors, many of them expatriates who were influenced by or leading exponents of the German Expressionism of the twenties (for example, *The Cabinet of Dr. Caligari*) with its emphasis on visual interpretation and evocation of tone and content, by the murky atmosphere of French pre-war films (for example, *Port of Shadows*), and beyond that by a strain of nineteenth-century romanticism.

Some of the prime figures among these expatriate directors were Billy Wilder (*Double Indemnity*, 1944), Otto Preminger (*Laura*, 1945), Robert Siodmak (*Christmas Holiday*, 1945), and Fritz Lang (*Scarlet Street*, 1945, and *Woman in the Window*, 1945). These directors, among others, made films with deliberately disquieting editing, low-key lighting and oblique camera set-ups. Similarly, their films were also often filled with rainswept foggy-night streets, shadowy figures, seedy bars, flickering street lamps, isolated coast roads and rooms dominated by mirrors; traits identified by post-war French critics as a genre and dubbed *film noir*.[20]

In addition, many of these *film noir* works constructed worlds where paranoia was the dominant feeling, and nobody could be trusted. A world where women were often glamorous and dangerous, seductive sirens whose every action was marked by duplicity and aimed at satisfying their desire for wealth and power. In contrast the heroes were frequently weak and confused men who were morally equivocal, and did not know, or could not commit themselves to, what was good and moral. By the same token the villains were often sympathetic figures whose charm masked malevolence and perversity and on occasion acted as alter egos or doubles for the films' heroes. *Film noir* also had its bizarre and seedy minor characters, its ritualised violence, cruelty, sadism, grotesquerie and sexual alienation and when the good triumphed at a film's climax (for it was still dominated by Hollywood conventions), its victory was usually an ambiguous one.[21]

These similarities notwithstanding, the *film noir* style still encompassed a wide range of works of varying quality. For example, there were films like Fritz Lang's powerful *Women in the Window* and *Scarlet Street* (1945), where a lonely, sexually unfulfilled male (Edward G. Robinson) was victimised by a beautiful, ruthless temptress (Joan Bennett). Moreover, the film was filled with notably vicious characters; Dan Duryea's insidious pimp being the most striking. There were also less successful films like Robert Siodmaks's *Cry of the City* (1948) which had a nice feeling for low-life locales: eternally wet streets, neon lights reflected in windows, sinister cocktail lounges, and decaying tenements. Similarly, it had some powerful set pieces: a gross six-foot masseuse (Hope Emerson) seen in close up devouring her breakfast, or through a glass door ominously striding through a house switching on the lights in room after room; a polite interview of a group of emigré abortionists, evoking the squalor and pathos of their situation; and the swelling drumbeat on the soundtrack as the film's totally corrupt and charming villain, Richard Conte, slips right past the police in a beautifully constructed escape scene. However, the film turns out to be no more than the sum of its carefully constructed and calculated tensions, a work of strong surface effects and style based on a banal, cliché-ridden script, and dominated by characters devoid of internality or interest.

It is much of this same *film noir* style which also comes to permeate Michael Curtiz's *Mildred Pierce* (1945), adapted from a novel by James Cain. *Mildred Pierce* charts the rise, by dint of hard work, of a housewife (Joan Crawford) from being a waitress to becoming the wealthy owner of a chain of restaurants in southern California. *Mildred Pierce* contains elements of *film noir* – stylish low-key lighting, seedy, smoke-filled police stations, pools of shadows, and avaricious, corrupt characters – and of women's pictures. These latter films, often referred to as 'weepies', were designed to offer women, especially house-wives, a cathartic experience. In them, fine actresses like Bette Davis (*Deception*, 1946) and Joan Crawford (*Possessed*, 1948) had to lie, scheme, even murder to get what they wanted. And although their themes of self-sacrifice, ungrateful children, or chronic and terminal illnesses were at times hopelessly soap-operatic and melodramatic they nonetheless featured strong women fighting for themselves in a world run by men.[22]

In many ways *Mildred Pierce* fitted the conventional pattern of women's films. It had a predictable narrative, tended towards overstatement and hysteria, and contained major characters who lacked even a hint of psychological nuance (for example, Zachary Scott's Monte, an aristocratic decadent heel). However, for all its lack of subtlety, it was an extremely suggestive work.

Mildred is supposedly an ordinary, lower-middle-class housewife (though Crawford never can convince audiences that she is anything but glamorous), who escapes household drudgery and an enervated husband to become a successful entrepreneur. Warned early that the pursuit of success and the abdication of her maternal role will prove destructive, she is punished by having her perky, younger daughter die of pneumonia, and by choosing to have a relationship with the feckless, parasitical Monte, who betrays her and lives off her money.

But her ultimate punishment is being betrayed and treated with contempt by her spoilt, evil, eldest daughter Veda (Ann Blyth), for whom Mildred has sacrificed everything so that she can become a lady. For Mildred, no matter how successful and obsessively self-sacrificing she becomes, never gains her monstrous daughter's love and respect. In fact, Veda is so pretentious that despite Mildred's success she continues to treat her mother as if her life has been irrevocably tainted by Mildred's having to work for a living. Thus, at the beginning of the film Veda's contempt for Mildred's being merely a waitress, and in turn Mildred's own embarrassment about her role, feels emotionally true, and conveys some insight into the sort of status and class anxiety that American Hollywood mythology of a social world of infinite possibility had difficulty in recognising and dealing with. However, as the film progresses the contempt that the idle Monte and Veda express for Mildred after she has become wealthy has less of a basis in American social reality. Indeed, a self-made success story such as Mildred's usually elicits respect, and though the idle and hedonistic rich can, and often do, bar the way to social acceptance of these *nouveaux riches*, they rarely carry the economic and cultural weight to maintain that exclusion for too long.

The film also can be taken on another level. Hollywood films usually treated career women (especially in the post-Second World War era) as people who had to be domesticated and made to see the error of their ways in competing with men. Even Katherine Hepburn, Hollywood's most noted feminist, had to accept ritual degradations (*Adam's Rib*, 1949) in her classic bouts with Spencer Tracy.[23] Similarly, Joan Crawford's *Mildred Pierce* is clearly superior to the men who surround her, but she still is enough of a woman to be manipulated by them. Nor does the film allow Mildred to pursue a career for its own sake – it is supposedly just a means to acquire and hold Veda's love. And Veda's behaviour itself can be seen as merely an extension and distortion of Mildred's success drive, or a demonic variation on it. In addition, at the film's conclusion there is a tacked-on happy ending with Mildred facing the future with her passive, dull, chauvinistic husband, who looks even more inadequate and passive when forced to stand next to her but, given Hollywood's conventions, is there to save her. To make this chauvinistic point even clearer the film allows Ida (Eve Arden), Mildred's intelligent, handsome, sarcastically witty friend who is also a career woman, to be treated as if she were not a 'real woman'. The moral here being that independent career women are lonely and asexual, and would trade it all for the right man. Nevertheless, despite the Hollywood conventions Crawford and Arden are clearly the most powerful figures in the film.

Obviously, Joan Crawford's career women owed more to the conventions of the women's pictures than to *film noir*, but in both genres women often enjoyed a great deal of power over the imagination and will of men. There were a number of possible reasons for the diverse and powerful images of female menace, power and maternal patience that filled these films. For one thing, female stars had a great deal of prestige in Hollywood in those years, and the films reflected that fact. In addition, the image of murderous wives and lovers may have partially derived from the American soldiers' nightmare of infidelity, and the Depression legacy of male economic insecurity. Of course the narrative, no matter how much the camera focused on the predatory sexuality of the female, always restored the status of male dominance by the end of the film.[24]

It was Rita Hayworth, a pin-up favourite of American males in the forties and Columbia Pictures' only major film star and sex symbol, who became the apotheosis of these dangerous females. As a matter of fact such was the effect of her role as the sexually aggressive *Gilda* (1946), that it inspired the US Air Force to place that name on the atomic bomb dropped on Bikini. Shortly thereafter she followed up on that role with the character of a mysterious sexual Circe in the intricately murderous plot of *The Lady From Shanghai* (1947).

The Lady From Shanghai, directed by her then husband Orson Welles, is a virtuoso piece of baroque film-making filled with aural and visual images and metaphors (for example, the symbolic intercutting between the film's characters and crocodiles and snakes), unusual camera angles and the rich use of depth of focus. The world it depicts is one of *film noir*, a dark universe of men and women who deceive and destroy each other in exotic settings such as the Caribbean and Acapulco. Although there are moments when the film seems like nothing more than stylish nonsense – all windy rhetoric and meaningless confusion – there is still the intrigue of the seductive Rita (Elsa) and the sucker in the plot, Welles (Michael O'Hara), a romantic innocent who is totally enthralled with her, and whom she plans to have take the murder rap.

Throughout, Welles creates original images and sequences to give a sense of Elsa's lethal charm. For example, there is an overhead shot of Elsa lying languidly and singing on the deck of the yacht, luring O'Hara from the bowels of the boat. There is also an aquarium scene where her face is juxtaposed beside an octopus, a metaphor for her predatory qualities. And of course for a grand finale, a playland sequence with its grotesque laughing dolls, chutes, masks and a house of mirrors, a labyrinth of refracted and reflected multiple selves. Rita is the omnipresent *femme fatale* whose snare of pleasure cannot be escaped, and though her image is figuratively and literally destroyed, and Michael escapes into the light of day, we know, as in many other forties' films, he is bound to her image for life. As he says: 'Maybe I'll live so long that I'll forget her'.

Statements like these only serve to underscore the despair and cynicism that were so much a part of *film noir*. Nevertheless, despite their sense of universal corruption they had little sense of society (though there were exceptions like Abe Polonsky's *Force of Evil*, 1948). But mainly they defined corruption in psychological and more often in metaphysical terms, where human beings could only stand impotent and helpless in the face of evil. These facts notwithstanding, as Barbara Deming suggests in her book *Running Away From Myself: A Dream Portrait of Americans Drawn From Film of the 40's*, forties' films (not only *film noir*) were seen as revealing a crisis of faith: 'A vision of hell in which we are bound'.[25] An insight which she qualified by stating that this theme and the audience's response to it were in the main unconscious.

Of course, just as much as these films may have on one level been a revelation of some unconscious public despair, on another level they were merely derivations from other popular arts such as the successful hard-boiled detective novels of Cain, Hammett and Chandler (for example, *The Glass Key*, 1942, *The Big Sleep*, 1946); and on yet another (like many film trends) they were products of whatever genre films made a profit at the box office. In fact, though a number of *film noir* works may have expressed genuine directorial sensibility, the look – lighting, sets, composition – seemed often to be more significant than their vision.

Even more interesting and perhaps ironic is that the existence of *film noir* served only to highlight the essential optimism of the 1940s. Despite the pessimism, cynicism and sense of universal corruption that *film noir* projected, both the film-makers and the audience were readily prepared, even desirous of avoiding their implications. As a result, even when logic and good taste demanded their opposite, the simple solution, the happy ending and justice still reigned supreme in film. Of course much of this had to do with Hollywood's system of self-censorship and genre conventions. On the other hand it also benefited from Americans' willingness to suspend belief. An attitude which profited to no small extent from the war-inspired conviction that sufficient energy and good will existed in the society to solve any problem and triumph over any evil. In fact *film noir*'s evocation of evil may have served only as a delicious contrast: making the ultimate victory of goodness and justice that much more glorious. Thus, though *film noir* did introduce the American audience to the darker side of the human spirit, that initiation was one that was more of form than of content, and one that hardly ruffled the basic self-confidence of the era.[26]

Nowhere is this outlook better illustrated than in some of the forties' films that dealt with social problems, particularly racism. Indeed it seems that a number of Hollywood producers, directors and writers appeared determined to extend the democratic ideals of the war effort into an examination and attack on racism and bigotry in the US. Films like *Crossfire* (1947) and *Gentleman's Agreement* (1947) were probably two of the first Hollywood studio products to confront anti-semitism as a serious social problem. For although many of the Hollywood moguls were Jewish, Jews were usually seen as secondary characters – often comic ethnic types in films usually dominated by an upper-middle-class WASP ideal. Therefore even when *Crossfire* and *Gentleman's Agreement* proved profitable no other film dealing with the subject appeared.

Crossfire is an edgy thriller, whose visual images and atmosphere are much stronger than its script. The film is filled with *film noir* shadows, razors so gleamingly polished that characters can be reflected on them, a number of ominous low-angle and overhead shots, and a psychopathic villain, Montgomery (Robert Ryan), who is a deceptively soft-spoken sadist, seething with feelings of inferiority, resentment and anti-semitism ('Jewish people live off the fat of the land.')

The film's strengths lie in Ryan's performance, and in its gift for evoking a tense, seedy night world of bars, all-night movie theatres, and cheap apartments, inhabited by characters such as Gloria Grahame's Ginny, a tough, exhausted woman, and her odd, pathological-liar boyfriend. The bitterness and venom that is exchanged between them, and the feeling that most of the characters are living near the precipice is more powerful than the film's attack on anti-semitism. For *Crossfire*'s social vision is a timid and evasive one, and in making the anti-semite an uneducated psychopath it distances the problem from the audiences' own experience and values, thus absolving them of any guilt. And in making the Jewish victim (Sam Levene) a war hero and an empathetic good guy, the film seems to suggest that a less heroic Jew would have been unable to elicit audience sympathy and concern. Finally, turning the homosexual victim of the novel into a Jew in the film demonstrates Hollywood's own fear and timidity (homosexuals could not be dealt with sympathetically in the 1940s), and its implicit belief that all social problems can be reduced to one problem, that there really is no need to deal with a particular historical and social reality because the liberal principle of tolerance will be able to encompass and deal with all problems. Compounding all of this is the film's tendency to be awkwardly and superficially didactic with its liberal spokesman, pipe-smoking police Lieutenant Finley (Robert Young), stopping the action and providing a generalised sermon about standing up to prejudice. An editorial which ends up by using the nineteenth-century discrimination against the Irish (rather than the more charged issue of race) as an historical parallel to anti-semitism.

In contrast to *Crossfire*, Elia Kazan's *Gentleman's Agreement* (1947), though lacking the former's visual style and tension, does examine and dramatise facets of anti-semitism which *Crossfire* never touches on. In its story of a WASP magazine writer (Gregory Peck) who pretends to be a Jew for six months it presents a gallery of anti-semites who run the gamut from raging bigots to genteel WASPS ('nice people') who indulge in polite prejudice, and to self-hating Jews who object to Jews who are too ethnic ('kikey').

However, despite *Gentleman's Agreement*'s more complex perspective on anti-semitism, it is characterised by the same intellectual and political timidity and superficiality which is endemic to the social-problem films; having a Gentile journalist face anti-semitism is an evasion of the issue since it makes it seem that there are no differences at all between ethnic groups, no distinct social or cultural history or characteristics to distinguish Gentile from Jew; and having a Gentile as protagonist allows the audience to become angered not only because prejudice is morally wrong, but because an 'innocent man' is suffering from it.

Needless to say, it was not only Jews who got a dose of liberal optimism from Hollywood in the forties. Blacks from *Birth of a Nation* (1915) on had usually been seen by Hollywood either as brutal savage bucks, or good toms and mammies. In the thirties two new black stereotypes began to appear, noble victims who were symbols of general rather than racial oppression, and 'tragic mulattoes' (for example, *Imitation of Life*, 1934), whose skin allows them to pass into white society. However, until the

1940s problem films blacks were confined to minor roles, and racism was never explored as an issue.[27]

By the end of the decade Hollywood began to deal with the issue and a number of films dealing with race prejudice were released. In one of these, *Home of the Brave* (1949), an educated, emotionally disturbed black GI, Peter Moss (James Edwards) is cured of a trauma (psychosomatic paralysis) by a white psychiatrist. Moss's character is in the tradition of the noble martyr, being a passive, self-effacing figure who embodies white values. Moreover, he is the perfect black to exemplify the liberal ideals of the film since he is a war hero and a successful professional who can be seen by the white audience as being no different from any white. Consequently, as in *Gentleman's Agreement*, Hollywood again affirmed tolerance and integration provided it was for blacks and Jews who behaved like or really were WASPs. In addition, *Home of the Brave* also defines racism as a neurotic problem – racists are pathological and blacks are oversensitive – for Hollywood there is no such thing as institutional racism, and almost no sense of how deep a role racism plays in the culture.

Nor was *Home of the Brave* an isolated example of this kind of treatment of blacks in film. In *Lost Boundaries* (1949) and *Pinky* (1949) some of the very same ideals and analysis are applied. Thus, in *Lost Boundaries*, produced by the documentary film-maker Louis de Rochemont, who gave the film a documentary flavour (New Hampshire locations and the townspeople as extras), a black doctor, Dr Scott Carter, a tragic mulatto, is forced to pass for white in order to pursue his career. He and his family live as whites in an idyllic New England town with only his children's gift for music hinting at the 'natural rhythm' of their racial past. However, their secret finally comes out when Dr Carter is rejected for a naval commission because he is black, and then the family is forced to deal with the mild social prejudices of the town and their son's confusion over his racial identity.

Well-intentioned as *Lost Boundaries* is, it is still limited by a neat formula which deals with a peripheral racial problem, one which ultimately fudges even that issue. For example, the black Carters who are supposedly passing for white are played by white actors (Mel Ferrer and Beatrice Pearson) in the Hollywood tradition of *Showboat* and *Imitation of Life*. This is of course done to create audience sympathy: 'isn't it awful that whites are discriminating against these refined, middle-class white people'. And most prominently in the film's concluding sequence, the town's Episcopal minister gives a sermon affirming Christian principles (that there is a screen of hate hiding the light of Christ) and announces that the navy has seen the light and has begun to grant officers' commissions to all people of all races. A sermon which has a magical effect, moving a number of townspeople apologetically to welcome the Carters back into the community. Here again liberal optimism triumphs, though as usual in these films the social and economic conditions of blacks (alluded to here in some affecting documentary footage of squalid Harlem streets) are basically left untouched, and all the black audience receives as a sop is the acceptance of one church-going, white-black family into white society.

In a similar fashion, Elia Kazan's *Pinky* also focused on a tragic mulatto (again played by a white actress, Jeanne Crain), but the film lacks even the surface realism of *Lost Boundaries*. *Pinky* takes place on a studio-set southern town, all wisteria and willows, and trades in racial stereotypes and clichés: an irascible but just white matriarch (Ethel Barrymore); a traditional, strong, wise nanny (Ethel Waters); a hypocritical, fat clubwoman bigot; and a lazy, no account black with his razor-carrying wife. By the film's conclusion Pinky has refused to pass for white any longer and affirmed her racial identity by starting a nursery-hospital for blacks. In thus rediscovering her black roots, Pinky's triumph is a personal rather than a social one. A victory gained with the assistance of white paternalists and one that gives no sign that the South's repressive and segregated order will ever be confronted, much less changed.

Looking at these 1940s social-problem films, their timorousness and superficiality seem, with the passage of time, even more blatant. Of course they were constrained politically by the industry's commitment to making a profit. However, in addition to the pallid, evasive and sentimental handling of social issues these films had little energy, style or dramatic life of their own. The characters that populated these works were usually impersonal mechanical figures, lacking any sign of internality. They existed as representations of social problems, and their actions were totally dictated by external forces rather than their being people with inner lives and tensions who found themselves in and reacted to charged social situations.

All the same, despite their timidity and shallowness these films must also be judged within the context of their times. For one thing they strongly suggest just how deeply an artistic and politically committed culture of liberalism had taken root in historically conservative Hollywood since the thirties (one shortly to be decimated by HUAC and the blacklist). Similarly, they attest to the economic security enjoyed by the industry which enabled it to feel confident enough to touch on previously taboo themes. Indeed the very existence of these social-problem films testifies to a shift away from the conventional Hollywood wisdom about social issues, which was, 'if you want to send a message, use Western Union', to an equally crude faith in the power of the image to produce instant social change. In fact the lack of subtlety and complexity in these films can in some ways be seen as yet another sign of the overwhelming optimism of the era; an optimism which refused to see any problem as insoluble.[28]

Fortunately there were a few films that were a sharp departure from this facile optimism. In vivid contrast to films like *Lost Boundaries* and *Gentleman's Agreement* was *Force of Evil* (1948), written and directed by Abraham Polonsky (soon to be a victim of the blacklist). On the surface *Force of Evil* is a formula melodrama about the numbers racket, whose gunplay and violent confrontations are awkwardly edited and devoid of dramatic tension. However, there is much more to the film than the story of a bad-good guy who by the film's climax is ready to go straight. It is an ambiguous and imaginative work which uses the Hollywood conventions to evoke on one level a portrait of American society dominated by capitalist greed and acquisitiveness, and on another level a complex guilt-ridden Cain and Abel relationship between the two brothers each caught in the coils of the success ethic.

Though Polonsky's characters are shaped by the social system and its pernicious values, they are not simply symbols or representations of a corrupt society. They have inner lives and psyches which are both shaped by and independent of social forces. In this poetic, small, near masterpiece, Polonsky has successfully fused Marxist and Freudian strains. The film's protagonist, Joe Morse (John Garfield), is a tough perceptive lawyer who is aware of his own inability to resist corruption in becoming part of the rackets. But Joe is able to rationalise his choices by discovering guilt in everybody else and Polonsky in turn does not allow any of the film's other characters to be free of guilt. The police, special prosecutor Hall, Joe's sweating, self-righteous brother Leo (Thomas Gomez) and even Leo's naive, dreamy stenographer, Doris, are tainted by the seductions of money and success.

Polonsky's direction is characterised by extremely long overheads of minute figures dwarfed by Wall Street buildings – a metaphor for monolithic capitalist power – and by the *film noir* images of seedy numbers parlours, opulent winding staircases and shadows augering doom. However, much more original than the film's imagery is Polonsky's use of language – dialogue and narration – which he aims to make play an equal, sometimes dialectical, relationship with the visual images. And though at moments the words become overly literary and self-conscious, its Joycean repetitions, city argot and inflection and metaphors (for example, 'money spread over the city like perfume') create a true sense of street poetry and set the film apart from almost all other forties' films.

Force of Evil concludes with Joe Morse descending on a grey morning to the 'bottom of the world' to discover his brother Leo's dead body left looking like an 'old dirty rag'. Polonsky does not have Joe indulge in grand gestures nor does he insert polemics for the class struggle or radical change. There is only a solitary Joe, willing to make his own understated stand, ready to help if he can. Polonsky's film offers no facile optimism; it knows just how powerful the capitalist ethos is, that it is not only Wall Street that has a gangster ethic, but that the whole American culture and consciousness is permeated with capitalist values and dreams.

Besides *Force of Evil* another film that dealt with some subtlety and insight into political and social themes was Billy Wilder's *A Foreign Affair* (1948). In this film Wilder displayed his talent for mordant, sharp comedy satirising the foolishness and naivety of an American congressional committee in post-war occupied Germany. Wilder is particularly nasty about American provincialism, ethnocentrism and self-righteousness, and also shows how easily their moralising is subverted when confronted by European cynicism and sophis-tication (though the portrait of the Germans interested only in self-preservation is not a very sympathetic one). However, as is Wilder's wont, by the film's climax he has thoroughly softened its bite, and has endorsed the American values he so savagely at first poked fun at.

Clearly, the compromises inherent in *A Foreign Affair* were the Hollywood norm, since it never had the courage or the imagination to deal truly with controversial political and social themes. It was much easier for Hollywood to work in genres which provided comforting fantasy images, such as the musi-cal: a genre which ever since its 'All Talkin', All Dancin', All Singin' ' days of the late twenties and early thirties had become one of Hollywood's glories. Though various studios vied for the honour of producing the best musicals in the late thirties, by the forties the undisputed leadership in the genre had fallen to MGM. There the Freed unit, with talents like Gene Kelly, Judy Garland, Fred Astaire, Vincente Minnelli and others, turned out hit after hit.[29]

Though often considered the most escapist of the Hollywood genres the musical nevertheless succeeded in striking emo-tional chords that few other films could touch. For one thing its tunes became the hallmark of an era. Thus Judy Garland's *Wizard of Oz* rendition of 'Over the Rainbow' became a world-wide hymn of a hoped-for post-war world of peace and prosperity. Similarly, the same film's 'We're Off to see the Wizard' became the anthem of the British Army as it chased Rommel across the sands of North Africa, and 'Ding Dong the Witch is Dead' was danced to the world over on VE day.

On another level the film's singing and dancing intimated a kind of energy that lurked beneath the surface of these films and seemed ready to burst forth at any moment. Most often during the war years that energy seemed to nestle softly in a nostalgic evocation of a turn-of-the-century America; an idealised world that was perhaps never better realised than in Vincente Minnelli's *Meet Me in St. Louis* (1944). As a matter of fact, except for the momentary anxiety over the family's possible uprooting because of the father's job mobility, some nervousness about whether or not the boy next door, John Truett (Tom Drake), loved Esther Smith (Judy Garland), and the Halloween night terrors of little 'Tootie' (Margaret O'Brien) the Smith family lived an almost Andy Hardy idyll; an edenic past of home and family topped off by a bright vision of future progress embodied in the St Louis Fair of 1903.

It was this version of a bright promising new world that burst into fruition in Gene Kelly and Stanley Donen's film *On the Town* (1949). The tale of three sailors on a three-day pass in New York, the film not only used real locations – the Brooklyn Bridge, the Statue of Liberty and the Empire State Building – it made the city into a magical place where one could realise all one's dreams, especially those of love and success.

Beginning with a long crane shot of a longshoreman on his way to work, singing 'I feel like I'm not out of bed yet', the film then cuts to its three sailors (Kelly, Sinatra and Jules Imunshin) coming off their ship ready to take on the world and New York. The sailors are innocents filled with a sense of wonder as they sing 'New York, New York, it's a wonderful town'. But have the confidence that it is all there to be taken, as the camera trails them while they sing 'We're really living, we're going on the town'. Such is the effect of their energy that it allows them to liberate three young women – an overworked taxi-driver (Betty Garrett), an oversexed socialite (Anne Miller), and a ballerina reduced to kootch dancing at Coney Island (Vera Ellen). As they make their glorious romp through New York, the city becomes a metropolis of grandeur, romance, vitality and sentiment (even the cops are soft-hearted), the symbolic buoyant capital of an even more buoyant America.[30]

It is this exuberant sense of energy, joy and confidence that more than anything else characterises the forties and their films. Certainly there were dark clouds looming, such as HUAC threatening to sap that vitality. In addition the *film noir* of the era had raised the curtain on a darker side of the American psyche and character. Nevertheless, for most Americans the forties – particularly the late forties – were the first relatively unruffled period of peace and prosperity that they had enjoyed in almost two decades. Despite the fact that there were fears of Russia and a native communist fifth column there was also the faith that America had both the material and the moral capacity to deal with this 'red menace'. By the same token, Hollywood had emerged from the war with its coffers, audience and prestige at an all-time peak. As a result the forties in Hollywood were perhaps the last time that there would be sufficient self-assurance there to be able to construct its own insulated coherent world, which could unself-consciously endorse the American dream. Undoubtedly, for most Americans and for Hollywood the forties were truly 'The Best Years of Our Lives'.

3. The Fifties

THOUGH the fifties began on a dark, ominous note with the US (as part of a nominally UN force) becoming involved in a war in Korea, and the repressive and paranoid investigations of Senator McCarthy and company in full throttle, the decade utlimately evolved into one permeated by a broad political and cultural consensus.[1]

The first years of the decade were dominated by the stalemated Korean War – a conflict in which the Truman administration was willing to eschew military victory for limited war and a negotiated settlement. Truman's military policies were challenged by Second World War hero General Douglas MacArthur, who was then commander of the United Nations forces. Cloaking himself in his own sense of omniscience and nineteenth-century patriotic simplicities, MacArthur saw Truman's policies as an appeasement of communism and committed himself to total victory in Korea. In response, Truman fired MacArthur for insubordination, and as a consequence subsequently found himself the object of intense public rage.[2]

That rage soon found a home in the McCarthy and HUAC investigations of a domestic communist conspiracy, which supposedly owed its loyalty to the Soviet Union. This conspiracy was seen as both threatening and attempting to take over a number of American institutions including Hollywood. The anti-communist crusade involved a variety of groups ranging from the American Civil Liberties Union (who refused to defend communists from 1953–59), and Hubert Humphrey, who as a senator proposed a bill to outlaw the Communist Party, to Senator Joseph McCarthy (Republican, Wisconsin), who opportunistically manipulated the issue to promote his own power and career. For four years he was extremely successful in using smears and innuendos to trample on individual rights and helped to create a climate of political fear and conformity.[3]

Interestingly enough, in the fifties many liberal intellectuals placed the blame for McCarthy on the left rather than on the right, vilifying the accused atom spies, the Rosenbergs, for their crude, middlebrow popular front style (and demonstrating little or no interest in the justice of their case), and at times even supported the general public's view that the rights of communists and communist sympathisers should be denied. But in 1954 when McCarthy went after the army and even dropped hints that President Eisenhower was soft on communism he overreached himself and initiated his own rather rapid fall from power and celebrity. McCarthy's decline clearly did not signify a turn to the left, or the opening of a public discussion of such issues as the admission of China to the UN or a willingness to talk about a social commitment to the poor, but it did mean a moderation of the repressive and divisive impulses that dominated the early fifties.[4]

The prime American political symbol of the fifties, however, was not Joe McCarthy but General Dwight Eisenhower, the Republican President from 1952 to 1960. Ike was a Second World War military hero, whose calm, avuncular, non-ideological presence projected a politics which muted controversy and offered something both to liberals and to conservatives. In office (though disliking the welfare state) Ike accepted the reforms of the New Deal without extending them, and was prepared to use fiscal and monetary measures to maintain full employment. Though also believing in the Cold War, and unable to distinguish between communist and nationalist revolutions (for example, CIA interventions in Iran and Guatemala occurred during his administration) he refused to engage in an arms race with the Soviets (he believed in a nuclear truce), and studiously avoided getting the US into war.[5]

Eisenhower was a cautious president, who though unsympathetic to the growing Civil Rights Movement, reluctantly sent troops to Little Rock to ensure school desegregation in 1957, and in crisis after crisis kept political tension beneath the surface. As a result, Eisenhower by dint of his confident cautiousness and political skilfulness was able to preside over a national political consensus which excluded only paranoid right elements, Southern reactionaries, segments of the old left and the few independent radicals who were still functioning as critics.[6]

This political consensus was built on and reinforced by an intellectual consensus shared by most American intellectuals. They held that the age of ideology was over (for example, see Daniel Bell, *The End of Ideology*) and in its place substituted an optimistic faith in capitalism, political pluralism and the uniqueness and perfectibility of American society. These supposed hard-nosed anti-ideologues had of course constructed their own ideology – building it on a belief that economic growth and the pragmatic application of social science principles would provide social justice and solve social problems. In their vision there would be no need for economic redistribution (many of them were ex-radicals who out of a complex of motives rejected their own political past), for the American people were supposedly becoming more economically equal, and poverty, during the rare times it was acknowledged to exist, was seen as gradually disappearing. In turn they also read the idea of class and class conflict out of American reality, promoting their own liberal mythology that in a totally middle-class society everybody had an equal opportunity. The other prime element of this ideological consensus was a liberal anti-communism (for example, *Partisan Review* became an avid defender of the West), which saw the cold war as far more significant than domestic affairs. This was a belief so potent that even the newly merged American Federation of Labour and Congress of Industrial Organisations gave more attention to the anti-communist struggle than to organising the mass of workers who remained outside the unions.[7]

However, though most intellectuals were either complacent about American politics or turned to contemplating existential questions in the fifties and simply ceased being political dissenters and critics, some continued to keep their critical skills alive by analysing the limits of mass culture. Indeed in the fifties the economy of abundance helped to create a powerful suburban and consumer culture where materialism and conformity were the order of the era. College students were for the most part apolitical ('a silent generation'), interested in a fraternity-sorority-based social life and in preparing for future careers. The Reverend Norman Vincent Peale, with his message of 'positive thinking' became the country's most popular moralist and preacher; the droning, folksy Arthur Godfrey became one of the top television personalities; and 'about four times the expenditures on public libraries were paid out for comic books'.[8]

It was this culture, often built on ideas which at best were vulgar platitudes, on an obsession with consumer goods and personal comfort and amusement, and on television programming dominated by the skilled slapstick of *I Love Lucy* and the greed and contrivance of quiz shows such as *Twenty-one*, which critics satirised and excoriated.

In books like William H. Whyte's *The Organization Man* (1956) and David Riesman's more scholarly and complex *The Lonely Crowd* (1950) American middle-class life was criticised for its penchant for uniformity, social role-playing and quietism. Other critics poked fun at media, advertising, the automobile culture and the anxiety-laden drive for social status and material goods. However, though the inanity and tastelessness of so much of television and the bland conventionality of suburban life were criticised there was no attempt by these critics to break from the political and social consensus of the fifties. They accepted the social structure that helped shape the culture, and most of the targets they went after were not particularly controversial ones.[9]

Nevertheless, despite the serene and confident veneer of the Eisenhower years, there were subversive currents and strains that though often unrecognised co-existed with the dominant mood of stability and complacency. For one thing, the threat of nuclear war shadowed the period, creating among some people a sense of fatalism and despair and ultimately leading to protests against the civil defence programme in the late 1950s. Secondly, though the movement to the suburbs by urban whites was viewed in the fifties either satirically or sympathetically – ordinary Americans achieving their small portion of the American Dream – the radical consequences of this flight (by 1950, 40 to 50 million Americans lived in the suburbs) for the inner city of the 1960s and 1970s were not foreseen. The departure of the white middle and lower middle class and their replacement by black and hispanic poor ultimately led in the following decades to the erosion of the urban tax base (built on the sales and property taxes of its inhabitants), the escalation of urban problems and even greater residential segregation than existed in the past.[10]

There were also other fifties' currents that indicated resistance to the conservatism of the decade. The Beat movement, an attack on the middle-class conformity and hypocrisy of the Eisenhower years and the elite literary culture of the universities, came of age in the 1950s. Led by serious poets like Alan Ginsberg and Gregory Corso and novelists like Jack Kerouac (*On the Road*), the Beats modelled their writing on poets like Walt Whitman and novelists like Henry Miller and on the improvisation of jazz musicians like Charley Parker. In their writing and their lives they emphasised spontaneity, personal freedom and spiritual exploration; and though they were never an integral part of a political or social movement their writings rejected racism and the nuclear arms race and treated homosexuality without contempt or condescension.[11]

In addition, the fifties saw the development of a distinctive youth culture accompanied by a new (though derived from black rhythm and blues music) form of music: rock and roll. For many older Americans rock music was too loud and overtly sexual, and often sounded merely like aimless noise. However, at its best and most innovative (for example, the rock of Chuck Berry and Elvis Presley) the music had an energy, freedom, and earthiness that offered an undefined sense of a new life style, which vividly contrasted with 1950s conventionality. Of course, by the late 1950s much of rock music's class and regional identity had been bleached out and transformed into the mass-produced, bland sound of Frankie Avalon and his clones.[12]

Clearly, these deviant currents and dark strains did not dominate fifties America. All the same, it is important to recognise that the era was more complex than the usual images and descriptive phrases evoking a time totally dominated by a passive 'silent generation'.

Similarly, the films produced in Hollywood also defied facile labels and categories. In the early 1950s HUAC once again garnered publicity by investigating the film industry, buttressing the already powerful blacklist of actors, writers and directors, and helping to create in their wake a 'clearance'[13] industry which could decide on the political purity of Hollywood employees. Moreover, just as in the late 1940s there were cheap genre films supposedly produced to purge the Hollywood image of any taint of radicalism. Thus, a film like *Big Jim McLain* (1952) used a documentary style including an authoritative narrator and extolled the FBI and HUAC while condemning communists more for their character traits and qualities (they were either criminals, idealistic dupes, nymphomaniacs or disturbed fanatics) than for their ideology. In fact, their ideology was never defined or explored. Communists were reduced to being people who saw human life as dispensable, had no room for private feelings, and were even in opposition to God and motherhood.

The most hysterical of these films and probably the one least bound by genre conventions, *My Son John* (1952), was made by a major Hollywood director, Leo McCarey (see, for example, *The Awful Truth*, 1937). It was McCarey who had distinguished himself in the 1947 hearing by replying to a question from one of the committee members about why the Russians had banned his last film (*Going My Way*, 1944) with: 'Because it had God in it'. Following this, in 1950 he joined Cecil B. De Mille in urging all members of the Directors Guild to take a loyalty oath. *My Son John* differed from other anti-communist films by focusing on the conflict between father and son rather than the usual *exposé* of communist crimes and conspiracies. In fact, the film operates most powerfully on a barely acknowledged Oedipal level where both father and son struggle for the wife-mother's time and respect. However, it is clear that what McCarey tried to do in *My Son John* was to pit the all-American 'Jefferson' family's communist son John, an unathletic, sexually ambiguous intellectual, played in his best insidious contemptuous *Strangers on a Train* (1951) style by Robert Walker, against his modest, down-to-earth parents (Helen Hayes and Dean Jagger) who believe in football, the Bible, the American Nation and the flag.

It is obviously an unequal struggle since the sullen, slick, contemptuous John is seen by McCarey as a monster and though the overpossessive mother is a mass of neurotic tics – rolling eyes, tense smile and flapping hands – and the father is a rigid, banal legionnaire, they are totally vindicated by the film's climax. This is an incredible scene that has the dead John (killed by communist agents) leaving a tape recording of a commencement speech which, enveloped in almost divine light, plays from the lectern to his former university's graduating class. The tape affirms his faith in his father and mother and tells the students how the communist serpent numbed his brain and led him to become a traitor.

In McCarey's feverish world being an intellectual is clearly a dangerous, un-American vocation, and redemption can be found only in the moralisms of John's elementary school principal father and the hysterical religiosity of his mother. For McCarey it is the heart and emotions, no matter how pathological, that will not lie or lead you astray, but the intellect makes you question and doubt and leaves you open to subversive ideas and the rejection of commonsense wisdom.

Nor was McCarey alone in this view of the perfidy of the intellectual. It was a perspective that was shared, albeit with greater subtlety and complexity, by Elia Kazan, who also played a leading role before HUAC. Kazan had joined the Communist Party in the 1930s, but resigned feeling intense bitterness and hostility towards it. However, he continued to see himself as a man of the left.[14] And in 1951, at the height of the Cold War, and close to the time he delivered his infamous co-operative testimony before HUAC, he made *Viva Zapata*. It was Kazan's first truly personal and structurally cinematic work (a film dealing with the heroic leader of the Mexican revolution), an intense film characterised by highly stylised and powerful imagery and lighting and a political vision which was open to varied and conflicting interpretations, a sign either of its profound ambiguity or of its intellectual confusion.

Nevertheless, at the hearings *Viva Zapata* was viewed as a sustained anti-communist film, and Kazan himself promoted it as an anti-communist work. What could be considered anti-communist in the film was evoked most vividly by the character of Fernando (Joseph Wiseman), a Machiavellian, professional revolutionary and intellectual. Kazan conceived him as a sterile, cold man – an anti-life force – dangerous not only because of his political opportunism, but also because of his lack of human connection. In fact, Fernando is a revolutionary devoid of any political ideology excepting a commitment to power (a common Hollywood conceit and stereotype). He is willing to shift from the political left to the right without a moment's hesitation or reflection. However, it is clear that Kazan wanted Fernando to be seen (despite the vagueness of his ideology) as the apotheosis of the Communist Party commissar – a man who could use and betray the people's demands and his personal relationships and loyalties to achieve power.

Kazan's evocation of the intellectual's power hunger is, however, only one example of the film's prime theme, the oppressiveness and meaninglessness of political power. For example, in one important scene Zapata (Marlon Brando) is depicted occupying the Presidential palace, and continuing both to temporise and to intimidate the peasants as the tyrant Diaz had done before him. Obviously, in this somewhat abstract schematic sequence, Kazan wants to demonstrate to the audience that power corrupts and that revolutionary regimes have sustained the tyrannical patterns of their right-wing predecessors.

However, *Viva Zapata* cannot be reduced to an anti-communist polemic on the lines of *My Son John* since it is filled with diverse (sometimes half-developed) strains which lead to often contradictory perceptions. Given this fact, it is understandable that the *Daily Worker* would have attacked the film for being Trotskyist;[15] that a number of film critics could condemn it for its Cold War anti-communism; and a great many people in the 1960s new left could love and embrace it.[16]

For *Viva Zapata* is touched both with populist and anarchist sentiments. The film is filled with images of the peasants acting heroically and collectively to promote the revolution. For the most part Kazan tends to romanticise the peasants, projecting them in static archetypal images and silhouettes as models of innocence and solemn dignity. But Kazan's populism also has an underside in the person of Eufemio (Anthony Quinn), Zapata's brother, who is a barbarian desiring the fruits of the revolution – booty, women and the land – without any other commitment beyond self-gratification. And the power of the people itself is often undermined by the charismatic figure of Zapata. For though Zapata can tell the people that 'there is no leader but yourselves' he is portrayed as a mythic figure whose instinctive nobility and life energy dwarfs the noble peasants that surround and follow him. The mixture of Brando's larger than life performance, and Kazan's conception of Zapata make it difficult to believe that with Zapata's death the peasants have become a populist force: the 'strong people that don't need a strong man'.

If Kazan's populism is bound by contradictions, his anarchism exists much more as a personal response, a belief in spontaneity and passion rather than a coherent notion of state and society. There are no hints of Kropotkin, Bakunin or some form of anarcho-syndicalism inherent in the film. There is on one level just Kazan's personal distaste for bourgeois repression and respectability and his ambivalence about success. And more importantly, in *Viva Zapata* there exists a genuine antagonism to political structures and hierarchies. However, in *Zapata* Kazan is more committed to the revolutionary image and emotion than he is to the political and social ends of revolution; more interested in heroic myth (Zapata heroically astride his white horse) and rebellion than he is in history or politics.

Clearly, *Viva Zapata* was not the unequivocal anticommunist polemic some critics perceived it to be, but nevertheless, Kazan did pay his dues to HUAC with his next film, *Man on a Tight Rope* (1953). The film was neither a commercial success nor a favourite of Kazan's. Filled with Cold War speeches and stereotyped characters it deals with a Czech circus fleeing to the West. It pits communist thugs and bureaucrats against the cosmopolitan life force and artistry of the circus performers. The communists are seen as stupid, petty and anti-intellectual, and they are committed to stifling all individuality and shaping it to fit the party line. In *Man on a Tight Rope* Kazan constructed a conventional melodrama, devoid of real people, whose main aim was preachily to propagate an anti-communist line and to help Kazan get off the committee's hook.

In 1954, however, Kazan's craft revived with his Academy

award-winning direction of *On the Waterfront* (a film dealing with union corruption on the New York waterfront). A film in which he also was able to justify his appearing as an informer before a congressional committee. In fact Kazan stated that: 'Terry Malloy felt as I did. He felt ashamed and proud of himself at the same time . . . He felt it was a necessary act.'[17] Thus, on one level Terry Malloy became a heroic stand-in for Kazan, committed to informing in a complex and painful situation (where he could be called a Judas for breaking the neighbourhood code of silence) but also where an unwillingness to talk could be viewed by an audience as an act of moral cowardice. In addition the HUAC investigations were partially sanitised by having the crime commission hearing in the film represent all that was upright and honest in governmental action.

However, in *On the Waterfront* the parallels to Kazan's experience with HUAC and the political and social significance of the film are somewhat overshadowed by the powerful and intricate portrait of Terry Malloy (Marlon Brando). Malloy is a mumbling, inarticulate boy-man who lives as the union boss's patronised pet on the margin of the longshoremen's community. He is an alienated, tough, urban wise guy with scar tissue over his eyes from his earlier stint as a prizefighter, who masks his vulnerability by upholding a code which believes the world is a jungle where your first obligation is to look out for yourself.

It is this character that Kazan self-consciously but successfully transforms from a comic-reading bum into a moral and social hero. A change seen most poignantly and concretely in his relationships with the fragile, protected 'good girl' (Eva Marie Saint) and his opportunistic lawyer-brother Charlie (Rod Steiger). Terry is a complex figure, for though his language is plain and simple, his inner self is bound by a profound sense of personal failure and lost dignity, by a powerful loyalty to brother and corrupt union boss, and by the mixture of tenderness and brutality inherent in his character.

By the same token, Kazan also made a film about the longshoremen and their corrupt union. And the film's cinematography, though self-consciously pictorial, does evoke the physical surface of a world of heavy mist, haunting boat whistles, seedy, bare pocket parks, tenements enveloped in clotheslines and television antennae and an omnipresent river. The film also provides glimpses of dock rituals and activities such as the dehumanising shape up, pilferage and loan sharking. But it is all more an expression of Kazan's sharp eye for dramatic detail than his interest in the social texture and dynamics of the docks. Kazan's longshoremen are never really particularised, they are 'more social masks than people'.[18] They are seen as a mass, first intimidated and submerged by the egotistical, vicious and crude union boss Johnny Friendly (played in a roaring, larger than life style by Lee J. Cobb), and at the film's conclusion following a bruised and martyred (though Kazan denies it there is more than a hint of Christian symbolism in the film) Malloy back to work.

Besides trying to vindicate the role of the informer, the politics of *On the Waterfront* are much more conventional than Zapata's. In the film there is little of a populist strain, for the workers are incapable of generating any collective political action on their own. And Kazan is clearly less interested in exploring in depth the nature of American unionism – the relationship of the longshoremen's union to the shipping interests and the political machine is barely touched on. For it is the character and redemption of Terry Malloy which is the centrepiece and most exhilarating element in the film. Although Malloy leads the workers against Johnny Friendly in the film's operatic climax there is almost no political dimension to his victory (there is even a little element of warning injected into the film with the image of a defeated but still defiant Johnny Friendly screaming, 'I'll be back', at the workers). Indeed the heroic attack against corrupt power and repression has become here a purely personal and moral act, for there is no suggestion that Malloy has developed a political and social vision like Zapata, he is merely a more alienated and resentful version of that classic American hero, the courageous individual who alone stands for virtue against those who would degrade and threaten our lives. Malloy-Brando represented one of the more striking variations of that anti-hero who was frequently to appear in the films of the 1950s.

Needless to say, *On the Waterfront* was hardly alone among fifties' films that either dealt directly with communism or indirectly with the ideology and psychology surrounding the anti-communist crusade. In 1951, with the advent of the Korean war, Samuel Fuller made *The Steel Helmet*, a crude low-budget film which on one level seemed determined to be second to none in its portrayal of the communist as the last word in bestiality and savagery. The North Koreans leave booby-trapped corpses of dead GIs around, kill innocent children and indulge in human-wave attacks which give clear evidence of their contempt for the value of human life. Nonetheless, Fuller, in his primitive anarchic fashion, gave ample hints that he was wary of all ideologies: finding fault with his American GIs' racial and cultural blindness; depicting his alienated hero Sergeant Zack (Gene Evans) as a cynical, sadistic, cigar-chomping figure, interested only in survival and untouched by the slightest hint of humanitarian impulse (except for his love for his South Korean ward). *The Steel Helmet*, despite its tabloid script and cartoon-like characters, had a great deal of bite and reality. It also gave evidence that the war film could simultaneously mouth and subvert patriotic platitudes, and convey that the anti-communist side was no community of saints.[19]

To a degree this flexibility allowed some directors and writers to use genres as a means of commenting on American politics. As a result in 1952 director Fred Zinnemann (*The Search* 1948, *From Here to Eternity* 1953) and scriptwriter Carl Foreman (who had been cited by HUAC in 1951, refused to co-operate and was subsequently blacklisted) made *High Noon*, a popular western which was clearly a parable about the Committee's attack on Hollywood. *High Noon* was a 'mature western' about an ageing weary Marshall (Gary Cooper in an Academy award-winning performance) who alone must confront a murderous psychopath and his henchman, who are out to kill him. This western hero has a deeply lined face, sagging flesh, admits being scared, and needs the assistance of the towns-people to help him face the murderer when he comes in on the noon train.

However, in *High Noon* the craven townspeople find a variety of reasons why they cannot stand up to this threat to law and liberty. The parson cannot commit himself to killing, the old sheriff is paralysed by despair, the judge is a smooth careerist whose only loyalty is to self-preservation and others just hide or flee from the confrontation. Thus we are left with the lone American hero who must face and, of course (for genre conventions still hold), defeat the villains.

High Noon is a skilfully crafted, gripping and intelligent film which uses cross-cutting and sound – an Academy award-winning score by Dimitri Tiomkin – and the rhythmic ticking of a clock (the film's running time runs parallel to this time of crisis in the marshal's life) successfully to build up narrative tension and excitement. However, it is a film whose images are merely functional, and whose characters are intelligently conceived types without any genuine individuality or psychological nuance. And the film's moral heroism does not quite translate into political terms, for the hero has no politics and the villains have no institutional connections. Nevertheless, in its commitment to individual moral responsibility and courage, the film did convey to some of its audience that evils such as McCarthyism must be resisted and could no longer be rationalised or evaded.

In its use of metaphor and parable, and emphasis on moral rather than political courage, *High Noon* (for all its boldness at that time) was a relatively indirect work.[20] In contrast, a film that dared to criticise American capitalism directly stood the risk of having its production disrupted by vigilantes and even if completed might find few distributors or theatres willing to exhibit it. Such a film was *Salt of the Earth* (1954) which was independently made by blacklisted writers Herbert Biberman (who also directed it), Michael Wilson and Paul Jarrico, and sponsored by the Mine, Mill and Smelter Workers, a union that had been expelled from the CIO in 1950 for its communist ties. The film dealt with the strike of a group of primarily Mexican-American zinc miners against a racist, exploitative and repressive mining company. At moments the film was crudely polemical and stilted (more socialist than social realism), particularly in its use of militant music, heavy-handed cross-cutting, and stereotyped villains; a clownishly crude and violent sheriff and his deputies; a callous pipe-smoking superintendent; and a company president who goes on African safaris. In addition, the Mexican workers are seen as spontaneous, communal and brave, and the film's heroine Esperanza (Rosaura Revueltas) is a shy, glowing beauty who conveys great warmth and courage.

On the other hand, *Salt of the Earth* projects a feminist consciousness unique (left or right) for the fifties. For the film deals with the conflict between the sexes on the workers' side, as well as with class oppression. The miners have never thought about the feelings and lives of their wives, who are taken for granted, traditionally bound to home and children. But as the strike develops, the women, who are forced to take the men's place on the picket line, assert their desire to be treated as equals. The men's pride and machismo is hurt, but eventually they begin to accept the change in traditional patterns and not only do they win the strike but they clearly transcend their notion of sexual identity. It is a pat conclusion, but the images of women gathering on a hill to join the picket line, and some men struggling with the laundry are vital, moving, and pre-date anything Hollywood was to do until the feminist-conscious 1970s and 1980s.[21]

Clearly, with its direct unabashed left perspective *Salt of the Earth* was an anomaly in the fifties. A film more in tune with the spirit of the decade was Don Siegel's *Invasion of the Body Snatchers* (1956), a low-budget, witty, science fiction film dealing with the subject of alien infiltration and mind control that pervaded so many of the science fiction films of the decade.

In Howard Hawks' *The Thing* (1951), for instance, a US scientific expedition is threatened by a ferocious monster they thaw out of a spaceship. Similarly, in William Cameron Menzies' *Invaders from Mars* (1951), a small boy cannot convince adults that Martians are kidnapping important figures, and placing crystals in their brains which will force them to commit brutal acts. Of all of them, however, *Invasion of the Body Snatchers* is the most subtle. Most notably it is Don Siegel's use of a matter-of-fact, realistic style eschewing violence for still, silent ominous images that gives the film its distinctive quality. Indeed Siegel creates a world where ordinary objects are strangely illuminated and people's faces are not, where light signifies safety and hope and darkness means danger. The invasion of the alien pods (a product of atomic mutation) occurs in a small neighbourly town where everybody knows each other's first name. As the pods possess the human beings, instead of becoming violent brutes they turn them into bland expressionless vegetables, who feel no love, rage, pleasure or pain.

It is these qualities that are responsible for opening *Invasion of the Body Snatchers* to a variety of interpretations. Thus, it could be seen as the image of a society where alienated people flee their individuality and seek refuge in mindless mass conformity, or more probably, the pods could be seen as communists, the omnipresent aliens of the fifties, who are everywhere conspiring to turn people into robots. Of course it is doubtful if *Invasion of the Body Snatchers* was perceived by its audience as anything more than a conventional genre entertainment film. Nonetheless, the anxiety, hysteria and paranoia it tapped about the threat of communist totalitarianism made it a perfect expression of some of the decade's obsessions.[22]

Undoubtedly, a direct or even an oblique commitment to dealing with political issues was far from the dominant force in the Hollywood of the fifties. Given the competition from television, and decreasing theatre attendance, Hollywood gave more thought to recapturing its audience. Initially using colour more heavily and then seeking out new technological processes the studios attempted to overwhelm the viewer. Processes such as Cinemascope, Vista-Vision, Cinerama, and 3-D were introduced, exploiting the size of the film image and experimenting (unsuccessfully) with the creation of the illusion of depth.[23]

Ultimately, the wide-screen processes led to a number of blockbuster films like *The Robe* (1953), *The Ten Commandments* (1956), and *Ben Hur* (1959). These epics were on one level part of the religious revival of the fifties, cartoons of religious piety and, more importantly, with their colour, crowds, chariot races and crucifixions they were the last great flings of studio excess (where 'only too much is really sufficient')[24] which allowed these films to exploit the vastness of the new screen.

A glimpse of the tragedy that might lie in store for Hollywood was offered in Billy Wilder's *Sunset Boulevard* (1950). With its story of an ageing, formerly famous and glamorous silent screen star, Norma Desmond (Gloria Swanson), plotting her comeback with the aid of a young ambitious screenwriter, Joe Gillis (William Holden), who becomes first her collaborator then her lover, *Sunset Boulevard* is something of a conventional *film noir*. Nevertheless, along with its possessive, sexually devouring heroine and its morally ambiguous hero, the film also succeeded in contrasting the old Hollywood and the new – not necessarily to the latter's advantage.

Though Billy Wilder and his co-writer Charles Bracket depicted Norma Desmond as something of a grotesque (also filling the film with references to Miss Swanson's film career, including a snippet from her independently produced disaster *Queen Kelly*, 1928), there is still something grand and gracious about her illusion-filled old Hollywood that is lacking in the new. In this new world, grasping producers dismiss the 'message kids' and Joe and the screenwriter Betty Schaefer (Nancy Olsen) carry on an affair behind the back of her boyfriend and his best friend ('as nice a guy as ever lived'). All the same, these elements of ambiguity aside, the main theme of *Sunset Boulevard* remains – what the drive for fame and a glamorous life style can do to the psyche and soul.[25]

Contrary to the cautionary implications of *Sunset Boulevard* many producers still felt optimism about the future, based upon the success of big-screen musical comedies, particularly adaptations of Broadway hits like *Oklahoma* (1955) and *Guys and Dolls* (1955).[26] However, these musicals, though commercially successful, suffered from ponderous and inflated production values and the fact that by the middle fifties it seemed absurd for characters to adhere to the convention of breaking into song and dance at the slightest provocation. Indeed the best musicals of the decade appeared in the early fifties and came from the illustrious Freed unit at MGM. These medium-budget original musicals included Vincente Minnelli's decorative and stylised *An American in Paris* (1951) with the athletic Gene Kelly; his sombre and witty *The Bandwagon* (1953) with the elegant and feathery Fred Astaire; and Stanley Donen and Gene Kelly's classic show-business musical *Singin' in the Rain* (1952).

Singin' in the Rain is a buoyant and good-natured satire of Hollywood's Busby Berkeley musicals, film premieres, star biographies, and the introduction of sound, written by the urbane Betty Comden and Adolph Green and starring Gene Kelly, as an earthy, warm, dynamic, ordinary American

Hollywood star. Kelly is as always brashly self-confident and jaunty, and in the film's title number, conveys a feeling of exultation as he stamps around in rain puddles, and holding his sole prop – an umbrella – embraces the studio rain. With its pastel colours, cheerful songs ('Good Morning') and acrobatic pratfalls (Donald O'Connor energetically dancing through cardboard sets), *Singin' in the Rain* creates a world where any action can be spontaneously, calmly and naturally turned into music and dance. It is a world where despair and doubt do not really exist and where the happy ending continues to survive. And if *Singin' in the Rain*'s plot about the transition to sound is a metaphor of the challenge that Hollywood faced from TV, it is also an indicator of just how much optimism still reigned at the studios.[27]

A much more melancholy and despairing note was touched upon by Donen and Kelly's final collaboration, *It's Always Fair Weather* (1955). In many ways something of a successor to *On the Town*, its three GI buddies (Dan Dailey and Michael Kidd recreating the Jules Imunshin, Frank Sinatra roles) decide to get together ten years after the war is over. It is a measure of the sour mood of the film that the three find that they have very little in common and do not really like one another. And although both Dailey and Kidd are better dancers than Imunshin and Sinatra there is very little chemistry between the three (even their bravura garbage-can dance together, though clever, has none of the inspired warmth of the numbers in *On the Town*). Also indicative of the darkening Hollywood mood is the decline of the benign attitude towards the world of media and TV, in the satiric pot shots the film takes at advertising – Dan Dailey as an advertising executive singing the drunken 'Situationwise' – and at TV shows like *This is Your Life*.[28]

Even if *It's Always Fair Weather* did sound this despondent chord and most of the films of the fifties lacked *Singin' in the Rain*'s charming breeziness, its absolute sense of being at home in the world, the era still contained many genre films that upheld traditional virtues and were commercially successful. For example, in George Stevens' carefully composed *Shane* (1955), a blond mysterious stranger in white (Alan Ladd) is befriended by a group of homesteaders and in turn protects them from a predatory rancher and his hired killer dressed in black (Jack Palance). In one sense *Shane* is no ordinary western, it is a self-conscious attempt to create a mythic West populated by archetypes; with the enigmatic Shane continually seen from the perspective of an adoring, hero-worshipping young boy (Brandon de Wilde).[29] However, despite its artistic aspirations it was a much more conventional film (*Shane* is not much different from the radio and TV hero, the Lone Ranger) than the 1950s westerns of Anthony Mann (*The Naked Spur*, 1953): austere, bleak films built around a revenge motif or John Ford's epic western *The Searchers* (1956) with John Wayne as the most ambiguous of Fordian heroes.

Despite the sense of unease that began to creep into fifties' film, neither Hollywood nor the public were still particularly open to works which took formal or intellectual risks. Exemplifying this attitude was the popular comedy team of the fifties, Martin and Lewis (*Artists and Models*, 1955), whose slapstick routines and Jerry Lewis' twitchy, idiot, victim's persona were not so different from earlier B-film comic teams like Abbott and Costello.

Just as indicative of this conservative mood were the films dealing with woman's consciousness and identity. As one critic reviewing the decade notes: 'the 50s saw not only fewer films about emancipated women than in the thirties or forties, but there were fewer films about women'. Thus, even in the Academy award-winning *All About Eve* (1950), a film which deals with a strong, ambitious career woman, the sarcastic but vulnerable star, Margo Channing (Bette Davis) sees her career as ultimately insufficient, as something separate from being a real woman, and opts for marriage and retirement.

In a minor role in the same film, Marilyn Monroe, the sex symbol of the fifties, played one more of her dumb blondes, a woman-object, whose sexuality is unthreatening, guileless and childlike. And towards the end of the decade, in films such as Billy Wilder's frenetically paced transvestite sex farce, *Some Like It Hot* (1959), she added vulnerability to her victim's persona.

While Monroe was more a male fantasy figure than a woman that other women could identify with, the freckled, eternally sunny Doris Day was one female who was capable of eliciting both male and female sympathy. In a period where being popular had become a prime cultural value, Day's persona in battle-of-the-sexes comedies such as *Pillow Talk* (1958), with Rock Hudson, conveyed a super-hygienic, wholesome cheerfulness. However, though these comedies were built on an extremely puritanical, timorous form of sexiness, with Day always the virgin, her supposed sexual innocence was less significant than her drive, ambition and spunkiness. In fact so potent are these character traits that as a journalism professor in *Teacher's Pet* (1958) she can even put to rout Hollywood studs (albeit he was ageing) like Clark Gable. In a sense, despite Day's girl-next-door looks and behaviour, her characters often had jobs and projected a tougher, more independent persona than most of the other major female stars (for example, Grace Kelly, Audrey Hepburn) of the decade.[31]

But though Doris Day may have held down a job, most women in the 1950s' films were housewives or women seeking to avoid spinsterhood, who found salvation in marriage. However, in one traditional genre – the soap opera – director Douglas Sirk made films which used conventional elements and scripts to make oblique criticisms of traditional female roles and middle-class conformity.

Working for one of the most commercial of Hollywood producers, Ross Hunter, a Sirk film such as *All That Heaven Allows* (1955) was filled with artificial studio landscapes, straight from the television advertisements, melodramatic fortuitous accidents, a saccharine score, and happy neat conclusions. However, despite the clichés that dominated the film, Sirk was a stylist who could use colour, light, clothes and furniture to express his sensibility and at moments transcend the lack of subtlety of the script.

If the young, passive, handsome hero of the film, Kirby's (Rock Hudson) affirmation of supposedly 'Bohemian values', such as the simple life, love of nature, an antipathy to snobbery and an uncompromising belief in one's autonomy is presented in a dull and simplistic way, the older heroine, Carrie's (Jane Wyman) choice (though conventionally defined) is to follow her emotional and sexual needs and break from the usual choices granted to fifties' and women's picture heroines. Wyman's Carrie not only rejects her friends, but decides not to be *Stella Dallas* (1937) or *Mildred Pierce* and sacrifice her life for her children. In addition, throughout the film Sirk uses reflections in TV screens, mirrors and piano tops both to evoke a middle-class world dominated by gleaming surfaces and appearances and to catch the heroine's feelings of imprisonment – an eloquent use of cinematic form to comment on content.[32]

Although Sirk's film was clearly no radical feminist work since the heroine, though able to choose a new way of living, needed a man to provide her with both an alternate set of values and a refuge in marriage, its rebellion against middle-class materialism was symptomatic of much less oblique works which rebelled against the complacency and conformity of Eisenhower America. In these, male stars such as the virile, angry Brando (*On the Waterfront*), the brooding, vulnerable Monty Clift (*From Here to Eternity*, 1953) and James Dean (*East of Eden*, 1955) played anti-heroic heroes who in different ways were at odds with the prevailing order. However, their rebellion was neither political or social, nor did they pretend to be artists, beats or Bohemians. They were simply sensitive, sensual and often anguished young men seeking to discover and define their identities. Nevertheless, in the process they did raise some doubts about the nature of American culture and in an indirect way expressed some of the uneasiness that existed in the decade.

Of the three stars, James Dean had the most profound effect on the consciousness of the young in the fifties. Dean had an aura – a mythic presence – and with his abrupt and tragic death in a car crash in 1955 generated a cult and became a legend. His film career was a brief one, but in Nicholas Ray's extremely popular *Rebel Without a Cause* (1955) he left a unique and dazzling mark on the fifties.

Rebel Without a Cause was less about rebellion than about the anger of Dean (Jim) against his middle-class parents and the world. Jim is a brooding, suffering, isolated, high-school student who hates his apron-wearing father's (Jim Backus) flaccid amiability and weak submission to his self-involved backbiting wife. Mumbling, slouching, hunching his shoulders, curling up in a foetal position, the tormented Jim is like a coiled spring ready to cry and rage. Surrounding Jim are two other pained, rejected adolescents, Judy (Natalie Wood), unbalanced by her father's sudden rejection and Plato (Sal Mineo), a morbid, friendless boy whose divorced parents have left him alone with a maid.

The distinctiveness of *Rebel Without a Cause* is found much more in its style and Dean's performance than in its script. Ray used a variety of camera angles, intense colour and rapid, turbulent cutting successfully to project the tension and rage that permeates the film. Ray can also construct a beautiful, sequence like the 'chicken run' scene, with its white spectre (Natalie Wood) in the centre of a pitch-black runway lit by car headlights signalling the beginning of the race, and the use of interior environments (a unique one in this case) like the planetarium with its images of the end of the world which gives the feeling of being alone in a vast, empty space to convey Jim's and the others' sense of insecurity.

Unfortunately, the film's underlying ideas and its script are much more pedestrian than its images. *Rebel Without a Cause* is a work which holds that the causes of adolescent alienation are solely psychological. There is a muted implicit critique of upper-middle-class status striving and conformity; nonetheless, the script's emphasis is not on social or class reality, but on the failure of families to communicate and provide understanding. In fact, the film even introduces an understanding detective who acts as a social worker (the helping professions, such as psychologists, social workers, etc. became commonplace in fifties' films) and surrogate father to Jim.

In addition, the solution inherent in the film is both clichéd and sexist, with the power of love bringing about familial reconciliation, and the submerged father taking off his apron, asserting his authority and embracing Jim. However, what is most memorable is not Dean opting for a 1950s affirmation of domesticity – shedding his asocial self for a responsible familial one – but those images of lostness, of being a romantic outcast and alone in the world.[33]

Rather a departure from this image occurred in Dean's third and last film, George Stevens' *Giant* (1956), adapted from Edna Ferber's novel, in which he played Jett Rink, a sullen inarticulate ranch-hand who becomes an oil millionaire. Rink is the only character in the film with the suggestion of an internal life; a tribute to Dean's gift for giving nuance and complexity to even this most seemingly stereotypical of characters. Although in *Giant* Dean continued to mumble and slouch, as the film progresses he evolves from a hostile, arrogant outsider, filled with resentment of those who have power, to a wealthy but pathetic power-wielder consumed by alcoholic self-pity, racism and the resentments of youth. Dean's Jett is not a particularly sympathetic figure, but the tension and energy he conveys in the role is one of the few vital elements in this inflated and trite epic about Texas culture and society.

However, in contrast to Dean's earlier films *Giant* does make some interesting social points (albeit they are built on a sentimental, liberal point of view characteristic of the Hollywood social films of the mid-1950s). For *Giant* is both a ponderous soap-operatic chronicle about a wealthy ranching family and a critique and even a bit of a satire of Texas mores, its materialism, anti-intellectualism, machismo and racism. Unfortunately, the critique is subverted both by the long shots exalting a mythic Texas landscape and by the beautiful and somewhat progressive heroine, Leslie's (Elizabeth Taylor) ultimate embrace of Texas and its ethos. Of course, her acceptance of that world after years of ambivalence only occurs when her stolid rancher husband Vic (Rock Hudson) displays his humanness and manliness by brawling for the rights of his half-Mexican grandchild. *Giant* contains no real political critique, Leslie does not want to give up her privileges or change the political and economic structure, she merely wants the elite to be more paternalistic (to sustain the values of her Maryland adolescence), and demonstrate some kindness to the poor Mexicans who work for them. However, she is bold enough to accept intermarriage and the film clumsily suggests, through its final shots of Leslie's and Vic's white- and copper-skinned grandchildren sitting together in their playpen, that the answer to racism may lie in the coupling of the races, the usual Hollywood embrace of personal rather than political solutions.

A film with more bite and tension, dealing with the same issues of delinquency and racism as *Rebel Without a Cause* and *Giant*, was *Blackboard Jungle* (1955). In fact when the film was screened at the Venice Film Festival it elicited a diplomatic protest from Claire Booth Luce (Ambassador to the Vatican) as exporting a squalid image of American life.[34]

Blackboard Jungle centres around a tough, crew-cut idealistic teacher, Mr Dadier (Glenn Ford) who believes in education and democracy, and must tame a group of violent young thugs. In true 1950s style the actions of the hoods are given no social roots or explanation, merely psychological chatter about permissive child-rearing. Nevertheless, these hoods are no Bowery Boy cream puffs, but alienated, resentful and vicious, especially their leader, West (played with an imitation Brando–Dean slouch and mumble by Vic Morrow). *Blackboard Jungle* is a perfect example of what in Hollywood passes for social realism and a social exposé. For instance, New York is reduced to a studio set devoid of any sense of texture or place and the teachers in the main are stereotypes, ranging from Murdoch (Louis Calhern), a cynic who calls the school a 'garbage can', to the frustrated Miss Hammond, who wears tight, sexy clothes and is almost raped by one of the students. The plot is also built on contrived, mechanical twists, featuring sudden shifts of destructive or cynical characters to the side of virtue, and of course offering Hollywood's usual solution to complex social problems – the concern and commitment of one courageous, caring individual, in this case Dadier.

Despite these discordant elements, the film was still capable of capturing some of the difficulties involved in teaching tough disruptive adolescents (it uses the discordant sounds of a machine-shop class and the passing elevated subway train to help evoke feelings of oppression). Moreover, the use of the first rock music theme, 'Rock around the clock', makes a connection between that music and adolescent alienation and despair. In addition, the film also raises the issue of racism with the introduction of the character of Miller (Sidney Poitier in one of his early, more complex roles). Miller is a sensitive, strong, intelligent underachiever, who at first, angry and resentful of what he perceives as a white system, baits and torments Dadier but by the film's climax turns into a noble hero joining Dadier against West and his allies.

Although *Blackboard Jungle* is filled with embarrassing clichés about the promises of equal opportunity in America – Dadier attempts to get Miller to continue to go to school by invoking the successful careers of Joe Louis and Ralph Bunche – nevertheless the film does touch on the reality of black anger, and that is in itself a positive step in a decade where, excepting *No Way Out* (1950) (Poitier as a middle-class doctor) there were no other films dealing with black consciousness and problems until Martin Ritt's *Edge of the City* (1957). And in *Edge of the City*, with Poitier playing a kind of longshoreman-saint who sacrifices his life for a confused, neurotic white friend, John Cassavetes, there is not very much of an evocation of black life or problems.

By contrast, in Stanley Kramer's *The Defiant Ones* (1958), Poitier plays an escaped convict (Cullen) in the South whose character is given enough bite and reality to show his anger at Southern racism. Of course, being a symbol of virtue, Poitier's rage is balanced by intelligence, tenderness, loyalty and courage. *The Defiant Ones* is a predictable piece of liberal poster art whose key image – a close up of two hands, black and white, manacled together – is an obvious metaphor for Kramer's view that blacks and whites are inescapably linked to each other in America. For Cullen has escaped chained to a white convict, Jackson (Tony Curtis), who is morally and physically much weaker than him. Jackson is an insecure, petty criminal, who dreams of the big money and lives by the Southern racist code. But it is clear from the very beginning of the film that Jackson will be transformed and that the hate between him and Cullen will be turned into concern and love.

The Defiant Ones, like *Blackboard Jungle*, has a great deal of surface excitement and even some dramatic punch – the cross-cutting between the convicts on the run and the liberal sheriff (Theodore Bikel) in pursuit is especially effective. However, in a similar fashion it offers simplistic social answers: the achievement of racial solidarity through the commitment of individual blacks and whites to each other. And there is no sense in the film of the complex economic, political and cultural dimensions of the race problem. Of course, integration is made easy for whites, because the black is Sidney Poitier, a charismatic, seductive and superior presence, who at the film's climax even sacrifices his freedom for his white friend. Indeed it was this dignity, this transcendent humanness, which made Poitier the one black star who was consistently successful and acceptable to white audiences. Poitier never bowed or scraped to whites, but he was so reasonable and humane that the white audience knew that his anger would always stay within bounds, and that there was nothing to fear from Sidney's characters. They were men whom only the most ignorant or reactionary of whites would abuse.

Later on, in the more militant sixties, blacks often put down Poitier's persona as middle-class, masochistic and liberal.[35] Nevertheless, he at least no longer had to sing or dance and roll his eyes to have his image appear on the screen. In addition, though Hollywood's handling of the race problem was neither bold nor imaginative, given the conformist political tenor of the time, the emergence of a token black star could still be viewed as a minor triumph.

Ultimately it was this lack of political and artistic ferment or innovation in 1950s Hollywood that allowed an opening for a creative stir to be developed by a group of independently produced films such as the Academy award-winning *Marty* (1955). Ironically, it was Hollywood's *bête noir* TV that was the inspiration of this and some other of these works. For along with the hours of dross in 1950s TV there were some splendid moments. Under the inspiration of innovative spirits such as NBC's Sylvester 'Pat' Weaver new forms like the magazine concept show ('Today'), talk shows ('Tonight'), spectaculars ('Peter Pan'), and the long-form variety show ('Your Show of Shows') were produced on TV. Similarly, producers such as Fred Coe and Worthington Minor created original live drama shows such as Studio One, Philco Playhouse and Playhouse 90 which featured the talents of newcomer writers (Paddy Chayevsky, Rod Serling, Horton Foote), directors (Sidney Lumet, John Frankenheimer) and actors (Paul Newman, Kim Stanley, Rod Steiger).

Marty was the first and most commercially successful of these films adapted from live television. Written by Paddy Chayevsky and made on location in low-budget black and white, it dealt with the daily lives of ordinary people. *Marty*'s major achievement was in evoking the tedium and loneliness that permeates the life of an unattractive Bronx butcher (Ernest Borgnine), who finally meets a shy, homely teacher and finds happiness.[36] Although Chayevsky claimed that his work opened up the 'marvellous world of the ordinary', Marty offered no profound insight into lower-middle-class life, and is merely a quietly sentimental story, with a bit of human truth, viewing love as the means to personal salvation.

It was *Marty*'s commercial success that led to other small films, the most distinctive being Sidney Lumet's *Twelve Angry Men* (1957), adapted from a television play by Reginald Rose. *Twelve Angry Men* is about the deliberations by a jury over a murder case where the defendant is a Puerto Rican boy. Using a single set of a New York City jury room on the hottest day of the year, Lumet succeeded in adapting most of the conventions of the television play by utilising close ups, medium group shots, tracking and fluid and precise cutting from sweating face to face to build a dramatically effective film. Lumet was also gifted with actors and a cast which included a combination of New York character actors (Lee J. Cobb, Jack Klugman, E. G. Marshall) and a Hollywood star, Henry Fonda, who provided a seamless bit of ensemble playing as the jury.

Twelve Angry Men is a socially committed work which raises questions about the nature of the jury system, and by extension the nature of American democracy itself. The jury is a gallery of social types: bigots, a shallow advertising man, a decent working man, a cold logical stockbroker and the hero, an intelligent, decent, liberal architect (Henry Fonda). Fonda must convince the rest of the jury members that what seems like an open and shut case is liable to reasonable doubt. He is a resolute man with a soft, cultivated voice, who ingeniously, logically and successfully convinces the other jury members of the holes in the prosecution's case. Thus despite the doubts the film raises about a system where bigotry, complacency and convenience (one juror wants to resolve the case quickly so he can get to a Yankee game) become the sole basis for deciding the guilt or innocence of a defendant, the film ends on a positive note, with the defendant allowed to go free and the American system of justice affirmed.

Twelve Angry Men's strength lies in its dramatic fireworks and its well-drawn social types rather than in the depth of its social critique or the psychological complexity of its characters. It is a film where the villains sweat, rage and bellow a great deal, and the hero is a totally admirable and reasonable man. Every scene in the film is neatly choreographed and calculated for dramatic impact, with each of the characters given a single note (for example, the old man notices details) to define themselves, and a significant moment where they shift their vote. And the social critique, though containing enough complexity to convey how ambiguous the facts of a criminal case can be, still holds that for our institutions to be just they merely need one good man who will tap the basic virtues of the ordinary Americans. It is the type of Hollywood fantasy that such vastly different directorial sensibilities as Frank Capra and Sidney Lumet could share.

Besides *Marty* and *Twelve Angry Men* there were other small films which elicited critical attention during the late fifties, such as Richard Brooks' *Catered Affair* (1956) and Delbert Mann's *Middle of the Night* (1959), but the small films began to decrease at the same time as live drama was replaced on television by filmed series. And although good, small, realistic films were still produced during the next two decades – *The Luck of Ginger Coffey* (1964), *Hester Street* (1974) – after the fifties there never again was a time where the small film seemed capable of becoming one of the dominant cinematic forms in Hollywood.

Of course the small (low-budget, no major stars) realistic films did not attempt to subvert Hollywood conventions or the dominant political and cultural values of the fifties. However, in the late fifties some films appeared which were critical both of the military mind and of the development of nuclear weapons – *Paths of Glory* (1957) and *On the Beach* (1959).

Of the two, the more formally distinctive and politically radical was Stanley Kubrick's *Paths of Glory*. Though safely set in the French Army of the First World War rather than in the US Army of Korea, and never explicitly questioning the reasons for the war, *Paths of Glory* powerfully reveals the cynicism and careerism of the French officer class.

In what was to become his characteristically dazzling style, Kubrick (*Dr. Strangelove, Clockwork Orange*, 1971) evokes a First World War world of callousness and death through sound (drum beats, whistles), camera movement, lighting and striking imagery rather than through liberal sermonising. The villains of the film (with their formal-dress balls and opulent chateaux) are the corrupt, privileged class of French officers, who treat their soldiers like chess pieces to be manipulated or ants to be casually discarded and slaughtered. The two prime villains, the calculating, subtle and insidious General Broulard (Adolph Menjou) and the neurotic, murderously ambitious General Mireau (George Macready) are totally contemptuous of the men (they see them as 'scum') they sacrifice to their career ambitions. Mireau watches the battle through binoculars (one of Kubrick's many devices conveying war as a voyeur's sport of the officer class) and hysterically rages at the soldiers' retreat. The advance and retreat of the soldiers is evoked in richly textured battlefield scenes which are the most powerful in the film. The battlefield is a nightmare landscape of craters, mud and puddles, littered with bodies, barbed wire and the wreckage of a plane, punctuated by whistling shells and bound by a flare-lit sky. And the camera keeps on tracking after the men as they scramble through the debris and smoke to their anonymous deaths.

The hero of *Paths of Glory* is the granite-faced, uncompli- cated, courageous and compassionate Colonel Dax (Kirk Douglas), who is at one with the men. It is Dax who tells Mireau that 'patriotism is the last refuge of scoundrels' and defends the three court-martialled soldiers (he is a defence lawyer in civilian life) who are slated to die as an example to the rest of the soldiers for their supposed cowardice (in reality to cover the general's mistakes) in battle. However, though Dax is a jut-jawed hero and idealist, the three soldiers are fallible, frightened men (they cry and rage) whose death is both barbaric and meaningless. And Dax not only fails to prevent their deaths, but remains part of an unjust system, which almost immediately after the court martial forces him to lead the exhausted troop, who are longing for home, back to the war and the murderous trenches.

Stanley Kubrick went on to make even more pessimistic films – where humanistic notions barely exist (for example, *Dr. Strangelove, Clockwork Orange*) but in the smug fifties, a film which portrayed the military hierarchy as moral monsters, and saw so little possibility of justice in the world, was a subversive work (and a commercial failure as well). *Paths of Glory* did not offer the facile, liberal solutions of *Blackboard Jungle* and the *Defiant Ones* or the leftist optimism of *Salt of the Earth*. It was a work of radical pessimism which offered only contempt for the conduct of war and the corruptions of power and privilege, and nothing more.[37]

In contrast, Stanley Kramer's *On the Beach* (1959), although it is about the world brought to the verge of extinction by nuclear war, ends on a curious note of hope. Based on Australian novelist Nevil Shute's best-selling book, the film was seen in some ways as a small step towards the easing of Cold War tensions (it was screened almost simultaneously in Moscow and Washington). Nonetheless, its tale of the aftermath of the Third World War and the last surviving American submarine which arrives in Australia just ahead of a post-nuclear exterminating cloud, seems nothing more than a backdrop for a doomed love affair between Ava Gardner, an alcoholic war widow, and Gregory Peck, the submarine commander.

Although Stanley Kramer's objective of making a film filled with stars which would act as a warning about the possible consequences of the nuclear arms race was commendable, there was little in the film except platitudes. Few people would take exception to the film's decent instincts, but only in Hollywood would bromides like the need to preserve the wonder of life be seen as socially significant. In addition, there is a curious antiseptic quality to the nuclear holocaust as envisioned by Kramer, especially on the submarine's last reconnaissance south from Alaska, there is no sense of the devastation that a nuclear war would bring (though smouldering and devoid of human life San Francisco looks relatively intact). Occasionally, however, there are moments when the film gives off a sense of the despair that might envelop the doomed survivors, particularly in a car race in which the drivers drive with a consciously suicidal recklessness and abandon. Unfortunately these moments are rare, and if anything *On the Beach*'s real purpose is revealed in its final image of a Salvation Army banner proclaiming the message that 'there is still time brother!'[38]

Ultimately, though intended as a cautionary message about the apocalyptic consequences of the arms race and nuclear war, the implications of this message might also serve as a convenient summary of Hollywood's passage from the optimism of the forties to the anxiety of the sixties. On the one hand it evokes the complacency of an industry that despite economic decline and political problems still went on churning out the same films built on the ersatz emotions, melodramatic conventions and evasive political and social formulae of previous decades. On the other hand, however, a number of these films managed to contain a deeper sense of uneasiness, an urgency, and a greater sense of the imperfections of American society than ever before. Of course, the fifties ended with Eisenhower in the White House and Doris Day starring in *Pillow Talk* (1958), but inherent in that situation was a sense of disquiet, perhaps even of time running out on a period of stability and consensus. ✳

4.   The Sixties

In 1848 revolutions broke out almost simultaneously in Paris, Berlin, Vienna and Milan which toppled long-established reactionary regimes and attempted to institute political and social reforms. Historians referring to this period call it the 'springtime of the nations'. Ultimately, these revolutions were crushed or gave way to even more sophisticated autocratic governments which were in many ways more repressive than the ones they replaced. Nevertheless, in their brief moment of victory these revolutions exposed some of the most glaring contradictions of their societies (most notably the growing, almost unbridgeable, gulf between the bourgeoisie and the newly emergent industrial working class), laying to rest the myth that Europe was moving towards a harmonious era of the golden mean.[1]

If some of the events of 1848 sound familiar to modern ears it is because something of a similar pattern of events took place during and after 1968. That year saw concurrent riots, insurrections and near-rebellions in the streets of New York, Chicago, Detroit, Paris, Mexico City and Prague. This '68 Spring' was also crushed in successive waves of assassinations, Russian tank invasions, police and army tear gas and bullets. However, like their 1848 predecessors these revolts also exposed a number of the contradictions inherent in their societies.[2]

In America, 1968 was merely the most apocalyptic year of a truly momentous decade. In that period the myths underlying the foreign policy of containment, the belief that domestic affluence ensured social peace, and the basic optimism that had dominated America's consciousness since the Second World War were buried forever. Indeed, for many Americans their image of themselves, their society, and their place in the world underwent a painful transformation. Moreover, despite the fact that it ultimately ushered in a period of intense social and political conservatism (whose force and grip on power has still clearly not abated) it left a hope that this was no permanent state – that social and cultural rebellion could arise again.[3]

Coincidentally, it was a revival of hope that ushered in the decade in America. Symbolic of that hope was the presidency of the youthful John F. Kennedy. Projecting an image of energy and eloquence which veiled his militant Cold War postures, and other political assumptions he shared with Nixon, Kennedy was elected on his promises to 'get the country moving again' and his prophecies of a 'New Frontier'. Tired of the malaise and apathy of the last years of the Eisenhower administration with its constant economic dislocations (recessions and unemployment), foreign policy disarray (U-2 incident, Japanese student riots, Cuban revolution) and missile gap myths, the country gave the handsome, cool, young Senator from Massachusetts a slim mandate (118,000 votes).[4]

In his inaugural address, Kennedy neglected to mention domestic issues but promised a renewed dedication to world leadership and proceeded to convert his mandate into a foreign policy of constant challenge to the Soviet Union and its allies. Ranging world-wide Kennedy and his crisis-management teams confronted the communists in Laos, Berlin and Cuba until they almost brought the world to the brink of nuclear disaster with the 1962 Cuban missile crisis.

Sobered by this flirtation with the apocalypse Kennedy negotiated a long-awaited nuclear test ban treaty, and raised hopes for further detente with a thoughtful foreign policy address at the American University in Washington DC in June 1963. Unfortunately, his assassination cut short further, more concerted attempts to bring about disarmament and disengagement.[5]

Corresponding to Kennedy's arousal of the public's expectation of a breakthrough in the Cold War was his seeming encouragement of the hopes of black Americans for some form of civil rights legislation. Hardly a radical on the issue during his Senatorial career, and barely mentioning the issue in his Churchillian inaugural address (one brief sentence), race was initially not a major Kennedy concern. However, equality for black Americans was 'an idea', in the words of Victor Hugo, 'whose time had come'.[6]

Ever since the forties blacks had almost imperceptibly made significant social and economic gains, and become more critical of racist and discriminatory policies and practices. As a consequence of their migration to the urban North they became one of the mainstays of the Democratic Party's political coalition and provided the margin of victory for both Truman and Kennedy. In the 1950s, the NAACP, which had diligently struggled in the courts against segregation and discrimination in education and voting, won a landmark decision in the Supreme Court against segregation in the schools (1954 Brown decision) and established racial equality as one of the prime and unavoidable political and moral issues facing the United States.[7]

What is more, the black community had produced leaders in the 1950s and 1960s such as Martin Luther King, Jr, James Farmer, Roy Wilkins, Whitney Young, Jr, Bayard Rustin, and the younger 'new abolitionists' of the Student Non-Violent Co-ordinating Committee (SNCC). Beginning with the successful Montgomery bus boycott, through sit-ins, freedom rides and voter registration drives, blacks made clear their demand for integration and equal rights. A demand which peaked during the Kennedy administration in the 1963 'March on Washington', where blacks made a highly visible, well-organised and disciplined bid to be heard, which culminated in Martin Luther King's speech, 'I had a dream'.

However, though the March was probably the apotheosis of liberal optimism and self-confidence, even in its midst there was the beginning of discord symptomatic of tactical, ideological and programmatic differences within the black leadership and community. Most fully reported of these episodes was the radical speech attacking the Democratic Party leadership that John Lewis, executive secretary of SNCC, intended to make, which was so objectionable to other members of the March coalition that it almost caused their withdrawal.[8]

However, even if the March maintained its facade of harmony, it did not prevent a northern black leader, scornfully dismissing the March's goals of civil rights legislation, from commenting: 'What difference does it make if you can sit at a lunch counter with whites if you didn't have the money to order a hamburger'. This remark neatly summarised the feelings of many northern blacks who for years had had *de jure* civil rights but were deprived of jobs, adequate education, and housing, and imprisoned in a psychology and ethos shaped by racism, that no amount of civil rights could allay or transform.[9]

It was this oppressive and tragic situation which propelled blacks into a series of violent ghetto riots that engulfed numerous major cities in the 1960s. The riots resulted in a diminution of white liberal support for (and in some cases a backlash against) the Civil Rights Movement – edging the movement further away from its integrationist philosophy. The move away from non-violent resistance and the emphasis on integration had already begun to take place in the face of continued violent Southern resistance (the murder of three civil rights workers in Mississippi), and a feeling that institutions such as the Democratic Party and the labour unions were hesitant about committing themselves to social change. Consequently, there emerged a number of militant, angry black leaders like Malcolm X and Stokely Carmichael who repudiated acceptance by and integration into white America for an ideology of black nationalism and separatism.[10]

Responding to demands that went beyond mere civil rights was the task of Kennedy's successor Lyndon B. Johnson. Johnson was a complex man of immense energy and virtuoso political skills whose personality and ideology of globalism were, however, ill-suited to the demands of the time. A Southern moderate, who in his Senatorial career had been more conservative than Kennedy, he nonetheless committed himself wholeheartedly to the task of civil rights legislation and indeed won the passage of laws that assured blacks of their rights as no one else (including Kennedy) could have accomplished. In addition, in an attempt to deal with black as well as white economic and social deprivation he fashioned a programme which he called the 'war on poverty', intended to be a link in creating for all Americans what he dreamed would be a 'Great Society'.[11]

Unfortunately, from its inception Johnson's 'war on poverty' fell victim to underfunding and administrative chaos, and to the politically safe but inadequate notion of trying genuinely to help the poor without changing the political and economic structure. The programme also elicited resentment and anger from white working-class and lower-middle-class people who felt that the government was neglecting their needs in favour of blacks. This set of circumstances became chronic and ultimately terminal as the US became more and more enmeshed in a futile ten-years war to stop 'Communist aggression' in South Vietnam, and the poverty programme in turn began to lose both funding and the President's attention and commitment.[12]

The war dominated political debate and policy-making during the second half of the sixties, and the assumptions that guided this struggle were the same as those that had directed American policy in Europe since 1945. These were that a Soviet Russian-controlled communist movement was seeking to expand at the expense of weak liberal-democratic regimes, and must be contained by the military and economic power of the US.

However, the principles of containment did not apply to southeast Asia and particularly South Vietnam. Here the communist monolith had long come a cropper on the shoals of divergent Moscow–Peking versions of communism, ancient distrusts, and even racial hostility. In addition, the governments that the US tried to support were never democratic, and hardly liberal. Moreover, the war was not a naked communist power grab but was largely the result of indigenous communists and nationalists attempting to wrest power from the hands of increasingly isolated, dictatorial, and corrupt neo-colonialists.[13]

Thus, instead of confronting communist expansionism the US was thrusting itself into a civil war. However, this meant little to the policy planners of the State Department and the Pentagon, who saw the war as a way of extending the Pax Americana to Asia, and testing their new military tactics against the post-Second World War 'wars of national liberation'.[14]

To accomplish this policy the government had to hide its purposes behind carefully built up subterfuges such as claiming that the US was helping the Vietnamese to help themselves, and by instigating provocations that inflamed American chauvinism (The Tonkin Gulf and Pleiku incidents) as a pretext for a military build-up. Indeed, as a consequence of this policy the US had over 500,000 troops in South Vietnam by 1968, and was spending upwards of 27 billion dollars a year on the war.

The inconsistencies and contradictions of this well-orchestrated escalation were not lost on a growing number of middle-class, white American youth whose commitment to activism and social change had been inspired by the early idealism evoked by the rhetoric and style of the Kennedy administration and the actions of the Civil Rights Movement. A group of them formed Students for a Democratic Society (SDS) in the early sixties and elaborated and attempted to implement a programme of political and social reform based at first on non-violence and participatory democracy. This 'New Left', as it was called, took the lead in recruiting and politicising an effective and dynamic anti-war movement numbering thousands of Americans (most of whom were far from being new leftists) repelled by the US conduct of the war, the growing number of American casualties, and the rising draft calls.[15]

The 'New Left' was the most politically conscious section of a larger movement of students, young and not so young men and women, who were not only estranged by the war but also were alienated from what they saw was American culture's spiritual emptiness and puritanical repressiveness. A product of the baby boom of the post-war era, the expansion of education, and the multiplying suburban affluence of America, the 'hippies' or 'flower children' (most accurately the counter- or adversary culture, since most of its most influential spokesmen were well over the dread age of thirty) gained intellectual awareness and legitimacy from the writings of 1950s intellectual radicals such as Norman Mailer, Paul Goodman, C. Wright Mills and the novelists and poets of the 'beat generation'. Nonetheless, the basis of the counter-culture's ethos was not intellectual (indeed, many were aggressively anti-intellectual) but the shared experience of drugs (marijuana and LSD), style (long hair, army cast-off clothes), folk and rock music (the Beatles, Bob Dylan, The Rolling Stones) and a burgeoning, assertive underground press (*Los Angeles Free Press*, *Berkeley Barb* and *East Village Other*).[16]

Though there were stylistic and intellectual differences between the amorphous counter-culture and the chaotic but more self-conscious and organised New Left they existed in uneasy coalition with each other. The coalition reached its apogee of political power and influence when their shared antagonism to the war helped lead to the elimination of Lyndon B. Johnson from the 1968 presidential race. They also were able to work together in the demonstrations and riots that engulfed Columbia University in the spring of that year and the Democratic Convention in Chicago that summer. In a similar fashion (though much more affected by the values of the counter-culture) it achieved its most 'utopian' movement in the communal experience embodied in the Woodstock music festival in the summer of 1969.[17]

However, both the New Left and the counter-culture quickly splintered as Martin Luther King and Robert Kennedy were assassinated and demonstrations did not bring the instant collapse of the Pentagon. Revolution-intoxicated leaders turned from community building and constructing a resistance to the war to nihilistic terrorism or sterile neo-Stalinist and Maoist dogmatism. At the same time, the counter-culture found itself usurped by hip capitalists and sensation-hungry media, who marketed and trivialised some of its more innovative and original elements. And the simplistic counter-culture ethic of 'doing your thing' was used by criminal elements to penetrate the milieu and exploit and subvert its ingenuousness. In addition the anti-work, anti-family, anti-patriotic, and anti-white working-class rhetoric and image of the 'New Left' and the 'Counter-culture' aroused an aggressive backlash which first manifested itself in the populist racism of the Wallace movement and then became a vital constituent in the conservative coalition that elected Richard Nixon to the presidency in 1968.[18]

The last years of the decade saw what was left of these movements destroy themselves and most of their appeal in a paroxysm of violent 'weatherman' demonstrations, the bloody Rolling Stones concert at Altamont, and the paranoid and murderous destruction of the Manson family. Also helping to bring it to the ground were the cunning policies of the Nixon administration which manipulated Vietnam troop withdrawals and an end to the draft (at the same time intensifying the air war in Vietnam and expanding the ground war into Laos and Cambodia) so as to give the public the impression that the war was gradually winding down, thus removing it from the national consciousness.[19]

Despite ending on such discordant notes the 1960s nevertheless had positive results. Among the most permanent of these was a revisionist impulse which stimulated many Americans to look critically at themselves, their history, and social and political ideas and institutions. Of course this did not guarantee that real change would come about, but it did make political and social nonconformity more difficult to repress and the simplistic pieties of the past harder to sustain.

Needless to say, nowhere was this tendency to ignore reality or bend it to its will more firmly entrenched than in Hollywood at the beginning of the sixties. Nonetheless, even in Hollywood the 1960s had their revisionary and transforming influence.

In contrast to the spirit of optimism which marked the opening of the decade for the rest of the country, the film industry was at its nadir. The most startling victim of that descent was the vaunted studio system, whose final demise was symbolised in the 1970 MGM auction of artifacts like Judy Garland's *Wizard of Oz* ruby slippers.

Taken over by financier Kirk Kerkorian in 1969, the studio (which once boasted 'more stars than in heaven') was promptly turned into a hotel-gambling enterprise with only incidental film-making interests. MGM was only one (albeit the most prominent) of a number of studios that went completely out of the film-making business (RKO), or became part of the leisure-time divisions of conglomerates like Gulf and Western (Paramount), TransAmerica (United Artists), MCA (Universal), Warner Communications (Warner Brothers).

Gone forever were the dream factories with their armies of contract actors and actresses, writers, directors, craftspeople, technicians and publicists. Instead the new studio head, who operated under the logo of the old studio, was likely to be a former talent agent (Ted Ashley, Barry Diller) who could put together talented packages of super-star actors, actresses and directors. By the end of the decade the studios were no longer interested in making films, they had assumed merely the marketing and financial end of the process.[20]

However, not every change during the sixties was an unmitigated disaster. Indeed, as a result of relaxing societal sexual standards and court rulings overturning rigid obscenity laws, the sexual taboos long governing Hollywood began to fall by the wayside. Gone were the twin beds and in to replace them came full-frontal nudity. And although this freedom was used by some film-makers as an excuse for sexual titillation, and even spawned a successful independent cottage industry of hard- and soft-core film pornography, it did permit a widening of the range of permissible film topics and gave American films the possibility of depicting a realism in human relationships that they had previously so sorely lacked.[21]

In addition to sex other Hollywood blind spots were breached by the protest movements of the 1960s, most notably by blacks who could no longer be totally ignored or merely cast in subservient and stereotypical roles. Similarly, the dissenting and deviant life styles and political ideas of the young, though they could be exploited and adulterated, nevertheless had to be confronted, especially since they had begun to make up the largest proportion of the cinema audience.[22]

An early sixties' film that touched on being a deviant, almost prophetic work, was John Frankenheimer's *The Manchurian Candidate* (1962). The premise upon which *The Manchurian Candidate* is based is the fifties' liberal conceit which suggested that: 'If Joe McCarthy were working for the communists, he couldn't be doing a better job'.[23] Thus, in the rather intricate, ironic script adapted by George Axelrod from the novel by Richard Condon, Sergeant Raymond Shaw (Laurence Harvey) comes back from the Korean War a Medal of Honor winner. However, the incident for which he was supposed to have been awarded the medal has been fabricated, and instead Shaw is really a brainwashed communist assassin controlled by his communist agent mother (Angela Lansbury), who uses him as a weapon to put her McCarthy-like Senator husband (James Gregory) into the White House. *The Manchurian Candidate* allows Frankenheimer to succeed in a neat, liberal balancing act, condemning McCarthy while simultaneously invoking the spectre of the 'red menace' and conspiracy.[24]

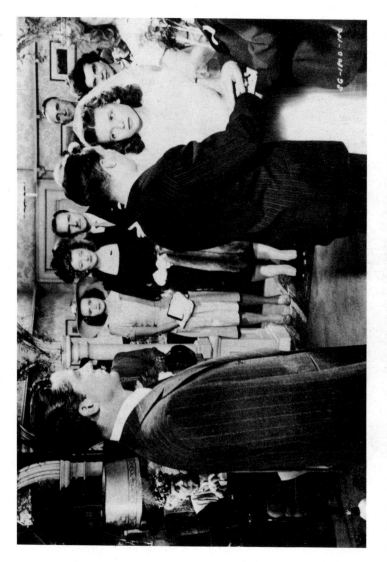

1. *The Best Years of Our Lives*: the marriage of Homer (Harold Russell) and Wilma (Cathy O'Donnell) — the affirmation of the American Dream.

2. *Singin' in the Rain:* Gene Kelly's exultant dance — the epitome of fifties optimism.

3. *Easy Rider:* Wyatt (Peter Fonda) and Billy (Dennis Hopper) on the road —
a film which captures some of the prime themes of the counterculture
and the sixties.

4. *The Godfather II:* a close up of a sombre, remote Michael Corleone (Al
Pacino) — an epic of dissolution, capturing how Americanisation turned
a murderous but warm and communal world into an impersonal,
alienated nightmare.

5. *Rocky:* white, working-class hero Rocky (Sylvester Stallone) fighting for the heavyweight championship against the black champion Appollo Creed — a seventies film which reaffirms traditional American values like the Horatio Alger myth.

6. *On Golden Pond:* Fonda and Hepburn as the aging Thayers — a conjuring up of cinematic memories and Hollywood iconography in the eighties.

Within this conventional, somewhat hysterical, thriller framework, Frankenheimer sought to create the ultimate send-up of McCarthy (albeit a bit belated since McCarthy was already dead and his power long since curbed) with war heroes, senators and even the *ne plus ultra* of American goodness – Mom – revealed as communist agents. He also succeeded in creating an illusionary, almost absurdist, sense of American politics (where irrationality is the norm) where plots abounded, sensitive souls turned into robot-like assassins, overwrought liberals denounced right-wingers as 'fascists', the right-wingers paraded around at costume parties in Abraham Lincoln outfits, and all figures of authority and power were never what they seemed to be. Indeed, Frankenheimer may have succeeded beyond his own expectations in creating a film of political prophecy. In it he augured not only the media politics of the 1960s with scene after scene dominated by the almost baleful gleam of the TV screen, but – most chillingly of all – its political assassinations, particularly the oedipal and vengeful Madison Square Garden shootings of Raymond's parents, linking private pathology with public and political actions.

Unfortunately, Frankenheimer's skilful, flashy (sometimes gratuitous) blending of fifties' political issues with prefigurations of the sixties' 'Put on' style (the calculated creation of an illusion to prove a point) and some of its headlines did not inspire a whole host of films struggling to illuminate American politics. Instead the key issue bringing in films such as Otto Preminger's *Advise and Consent* (1962) and Franklin Schaffner's version of Gore Vidal's cynical, literate novel *The Best Man* (1964) with its political convention-battling between Stevensonian and Nixonian candidates, was homosexuality.

However, there was more to *Advise and Consent* than its lurid, prurient treatment of homosexuality. In his cool, objective and lucid style – filled with long takes and fluid tracks and pans – Preminger was able to evoke successfully the atmosphere of the Senate and its rules. And it is these rules which Preminger endorses, for the film is a paean to the Senate ('The Club') and the American system's gift for compromise and flexibility, which supposedly transcends all ideological positions, and is ultimately able to control all opportunists and ideologists who wish to undermine its sacred procedures and processes.

Nevertheless, Preminger's complacency about the American government was supplanted by films dealing with the apocalyptic terror aroused by the thought of nuclear attack and annihilation. Frankenheimer also dealt with this issue (albeit indirectly) in his film *Seven Days in May* (1964), which was about a thwarted military coup prompted by the discontent of Pentagon right-wingers over the signing of a nuclear treaty with the Soviets. But its vision of the US as some kind of banana republic failed to impress the public.

In contrast films about nuclear war which in the words of Susan Sontag struck the audience's 'imagination of disaster',[25] their sense of participation, 'in the fantasy of living through one's own death and more the death of cities, the destruction of humanity itself', gained wide popularity. It was this quality that certainly contributed to the success of *Fail Safe* (1964) and *Dr. Strangelove: Or How I Stopped Worrying and Learned to Love the Bomb* (1964).

Unlike *Dr. Strangelove*, released earlier that year, *Fail Safe*, adapted from a best-seller by Eugene Burdick and Harvey Wheeler, saw nuclear disaster as resulting from the probable malfunctioning of nuclear weaponry's safe-guarding technology, rather than from the actions of paranoid generals. In *Fail Safe* it is just such a technological breakdown which launches American bombers on a full-scale attack of the Soviet Union.

Hoping to avert a catastrophe the decent American President (Henry Fonda) negotiates with the Russian Premier over the hot-line. However, one bomber does get through to bomb Moscow, and the American President winds up trading the destruction of New York for the Russian capital. Despite this rather far-fetched conclusion, Sidney Lumet's semi-documentary approach and his powerful final montage of the destructions of New York and Moscow fill the screen with terrifying images.

However, some of the most memorable moments of the film are the images of Henry Fonda shown in almost total isolation trying in his characteristic dry, almost laconic, tones to assure the Russians that it was all a mistake or shedding a tear after hearing the shrill sound of the telephone that signals the bomb exploding in Moscow. In these scenes we get the sense of an unbearable and unspeakable tragedy hanging in the balance as one man, against terrible and imponderable odds, tries to reason with another and discovers what a nuclear arms policy has wrought.

Fail Safe is a cautionary film about an out-of-control technology which makes men its pawns and disciples. And though it is not a particularly subtle film and either subordinates its characters to its theme or has them indulge in melodramatics, it does have in Walter Matthau's overstated, Dr Strangelove-like, political science professor a character who has genuine political substance. Lumet is a liberal, and he uses Matthau to represent the 1960s Cold War intellectuals (Kahn, Teller) who displayed their sense of *realpolitik* and machismo fantasies by 'thinking about the unthinkable'. These were professors who could talk casually and obsessively about building advanced weaponry and the possibilities and necessary risks of nuclear warfare, without any moral or humane constraints or qualms about the consequences of these policies.[26]

It is this assault on murderous *realpolitik* which was one of the prime themes of Stanley Kubrick's sardonic black comedy, *Dr. Strangelove*. The director of one critically acclaimed anti-war film, *Paths of Glory* (1957), Kubrick had long been interested in the problem of nuclear war and its effects. Deciding to do a film about it, he tried to adapt Peter George's novel *Red Alert* (*Hour of Doom* in the UK). However, each time he attempted to get something down it seemed more and more 'ridiculous' and he decided to do a black comic picture instead.

For the film Kubrick was able to enlist the mimic comic talents of Peter Sellers, who played three roles (the stiff-upper-lipped British Group Captain Mandrake, the balding, literally egg-headed, President Merkin Muffley, and the bizarre, Nazi-refugee scientist Dr Strangelove). In addition, he blended the talents of George C. Scott as the General Curtis Lemay-like, adolescent, gravelly-voiced, platitude-spouting, Air Force Chief-of-Staff, Buck Turgidson, and the dead-pan of Sterling Hayden's mad, grim, General Jack D. Ripper, the man who initiates the unauthorised bomber raid.

Complementing this ensemble acting was Kubrick's genius for creating striking images and settings. This gift is sustained from the opening scene where the B-52 is seen copulating with its refuelling plane (to 'Try a Little Tenderness' on the sound track), to the black-comic final scene where the doomsday mechanism has exploded and what results is a void with only mushroom clouds filling it, and on the sound track Vera Lynn is heard singing the Second World War favourite, 'We'll Meet Again'. There are also three settings that Kubrick cross-cuts from in the film: the extremely realistic and intricate looking technology of the B-52 cockpit; the war room in Washington whose flashing lights, big board, and large circular table skirt the line between realism and surrealism; and Burpleson Air Force Base where the psychopathic General Ripper is shot in tight close ups from a low angle, and his troops' violent defence of the base against other American troops is powerfully shot in *cinéma vérité*, documentary style. Kubrick also successfully uses sight gags like 'The Peace is Our Profession' sign at the air base, and the 'Hi There' lettered on the nuclear bomb in the B-52, and ironically juxtaposes popular songs with his often horrendous images.

All of these elements came together in a plot which deals with the destruction of the world by a Soviet-constructed doomsday machine ignited by a nuclear attack launched by General Jack D. Ripper. The attack is initiated because he fears that the nation's sexual potency is on the brink of being undermined by a communist-inspired plot to fluoridate the American water supply. Terry Southern's antic screenplay served Kubrick well in satirising a world of well-meaning but ineffectual liberal politicians, war-mongering generals, espionage-obsessed Russian ambassadors, and nuclear-war strategists.

Nevertheless, it went beyond poking fun at Curtis Lemay's, Herman Kahn's and Henry Kissinger's thinking on limited nuclear war, and revealed how closely their ideas were linked to the primal instincts of sex and death, with the President of the US talking over the hot line from his crypt-like war room to a dim, drunken Russian Premier Kissoff dallying with his mistress, Turgidson in turn getting calls from his mistress in the midst of a war-room discussion and Colonel Kong (Slim Pickens) astride the B-52's nuclear bomb (looking like a monstrous phallus) as it descends to penetrate and destroy the Soviet Union and the world.

Of course the humanistic tradition presumes that the forces that kindle these passions can be held in check by reason. However, *Dr. Strangelove*'s most caustic barbs are aimed not only at the deadly logic of thinking about the unthinkable, but at sweet, liberal reason itself. Time after time, as we hear President Muffley's bland, decent conversations with the Russian Premier ('Now Dimitri, you know how we've always talked about the possibility of something going wrong with the bomb – the bomb, Dimitri, the hydrogen bomb') or his shout as the Russian ambassador wrestles with the Air Force Chief of Staff on the floor of the war room ('Please gentlemen, you can't fight here, this is the war room'), we are reminded of the limits of reason and its inability and inadequacy to cope with the enormity of the forces it has unleashed.[27]

In fact, Kubrick does not posit any alternative to this insane world whose leaders are either ineffectual, stupid, infantile or obsessional personalities. There is no plea for sanity or belief in social change inherent in this film. There is only the monstrous Dr Strangelove – the personification of scientific reason gone amuck, with his self-propelled Nazi-saluting arm, his belief in the divinity of computers, and his gleeful plans for a post-nuclear holocaust society of subterranean polygamy (the ultimate expression of America's obsession with macho potency and power) – who emerges as a brilliant parody of the worst strains in American politics and culture.

In allowing us to take this black-comic peek at the apocalypse, Kubrick succeeded more in creating an inoculation against the fear of annihilation than in providing an antidote for it. Kubrick's world is a hopeless one, and as Pauline Kael wrote in her review of *Dr. Strangelove*, 'What may have been laughed to death was not war, but some action about it'.[28]

Despite this sort of criticism, Kubrick was able to create a film that summed up the anxieties about nuclear disaster which had haunted the fifties, and almost turned into a reality in the sixties with the Cuban missile crisis. Moreover, the film also was such a break with the shibboleths of the Cold War that Lewis Mumford, writing in the *New York Times*, declared it: 'The first break in the cold war trance that has so long held this country in its rigid grip'.[29]

However, *Dr. Strangelove*'s breakthrough was hardly exploited by the film industry, instead it preferred to grind out its usual quota of genre films led by the Cold-War-inspired, super-spy exploits of James Bond and his imitators like *Our Man Flint* (1966) and the Matt Helm series (*The Silencers*, 1966, *Murderers Row*, 1966, *The Ambushers*, 1967). Occasionally, these films were buttressed by a prestige picture like the nominally anti-Nazi but essentially Grand Hotelish *Ship of Fools* (1965), or the theatrical, message-bloated *A Man For All Seasons* (1966), or Sidney Lumet's *The Pawnbroker* (1965), a self-conscious, over-emphatic but sometimes moving work. *The Pawnbroker* centres on a haunted, coldly impassive, concentration-camp survivor (Rod Steiger) who owns a pawnshop among the violent, broken and defeated in New York's East Harlem. Influenced by Alain Resnais' *Hiroshima Mon Amour*, the film indulges in a great deal of parallel cutting from the garbage-laden ghetto streets to memory images of the concentration camp, but the attempt to equate the camps with East Harlem blurs the social and historical reality of both experiences.

However, even if *The Pawnbroker* fails genuinely to illuminate American urban reality it was more in step with the contemporary social scene than most of the Hollywood products. Just how far out of step Hollywood was could be seen in the films which focused on black life, for despite the Civil Rights Movement there had been no great surge in the direction of making films about blacks or black life in the late fifties and early sixties. However, in films like *Edge of the City* (1957), *The Defiant Ones* (1958) and *Raisin in the Sun* (1962) there was an attempt at least to portray blacks in a positive manner, to wrestle with some real, social and economic issues (especially in *Raisin in the Sun*), but all within the context of an optimistic, integrationist philosophy. These were films that implicitly and at moments explicitly endorsed the American dream of equity for all.

Despite the fact that the fantasy of equity and integration was being destroyed no further away from Hollywood than the streets of Watts, the film industry still clung tenaciously to its sentimental and simplistic beliefs. Nowhere was this more evident than in Stanley Kramer's *Guess Who's Coming to Dinner* (1967). Kramer's liberal credentials were already well established with his portentous, social-problem productions of the anti-racial prejudice such as *Home of the Brave* (1949), the anti-Nazi *Judgment at Nuremburg* (1961), *Ship of Fools*, and *The Defiant Ones*. In the glossy *Guess Who's Coming to Dinner* Kramer and scriptwriter William Rose decided to tackle the subject of inter-racial marriage.

However, tackle seems hardly the right word since rarely has there been such a field of straw men and women. To begin with the black male lead was Sidney Poitier, who had already established himself as a worthy missionary to white folks in a large number of films (for example, *Lilies of the Field*, 1963, *A Patch of Blue*, 1965) and in this film was a brilliant doctor, handsome, chaste and charming, well on his way to someday winning the Nobel prize. In fact, he seemed too good a catch for the innocent, simpering daughter (Katherine Houghton) of liberal millionaire presslord Matt Drayton (Spencer Tracy) and his feisty, gallery-owning wife, Christina (Katherine Hepburn).

Although there are objections to the marriage, ranging from the bigoted snobbishness of one of Christina's art gallery employees to the comic protests of the Drayton's cute black maid ('civil rights is one thing, but this here's another!'), they are brushed aside. Less easily swept away are the more serious doubts expressed by Matt Drayton about the social problems the young couple will be facing. However, even his reasonable concerns are effectively by-passed by Beah Richard's (Poitier's mother in the film) suggestion that it is not race that is preventing the marriage, but the fact that he and her husband (who also opposes the match) have forgotten what it was like to be young.

As a result, what emerges as a prime issue in *Guess Who's Coming to Dinner* is not race, but the clash of generations. A situation that is immediately rectified in Tracy's valedictory to Christina, about love conquering all, which is as much a commentary on his own twenty-seven-year relationship with Hepburn as it is to his fictional wife since Tracy was to die within weeks of the conclusion of the film.[30]

And though the issue of the generation gap feels totally bogus, especially in a film ostensibly dealing with the complex issue of intermarriage (not to mention the total blindness and irrelevance of the film's liberal, integrationist impulses to the rage and despair of the black community), it nevertheless superficially touched on something significant, the growing polarisation between generations. It was the polarisation resulting from the Vietnam war and the rise of the New Left and counter-culture which intensified in America in the late 1960s.

Already the coming of the young into American politics had been celebrated in the prose of authors such as Norman Mailer who saw them as 'those mad middle class children with their lobotomies from sin . . . their innocence, their lust for the apocalypse'.[31] However, they had still not forged their image in film, nor would they until Arthur Penn's *Bonnie and Clyde* (1967).

Bonnie and Clyde not only shifted the focus of film to the young, it also defined a unique sixties' cinema and sensibility in ways that *The Manchurian Candidate* and *Dr. Strangelove* had only hinted at. Perhaps the best indicator of how far it went in accomplishing this was the vehemence of the attacks on it by the critical establishment, led by *New York Times* critic Bosley Crowther. Nevertheless, audiences flocked to it, copied its clothing styles, and made it one of the year's top grossers.

However, vindicating the judgment of audiences over film critics is only one of the film's minor achievements. Its most significant successes were in introducing the ideas and techniques of the French 'New Wave' into the Hollywood mainstream, and in firmly fixing the gaze of American film-makers on the lives and styles of the alienated and discontented.

Written by two young *Esquire* writers, David Newman and Robert Benton, it was originally seen by them as a possible project for either François Truffaut or Jean-Luc Godard, a hope based on their appreciation of the French New Wave's understanding of the poetry and mythic nature of the American genre film. However, neither director was available, and the film was ultimately produced by Warren Beatty and directed by Arthur Penn.

Penn had also been influenced by the New Wave so little was really lost by the change, and he was able to incorporate many of their techniques into the film. Thus, along with free-intercutting of time and space, the use of slow and accelerated motion, he also used little vignettes ending in visual and verbal puns à la Truffaut and the alternating of comic and violent moments apropos of Godard.

These techniques updated a story that Hollywood had done before by Fritz Lang (*You Only Live Once*, 1937) and Nicholas Ray (*They Drive by Night*, 1949). Yet this classic tale of two youthful outsiders who take to a life of crime in an unjust society held a powerful attraction for an audience who also felt outside the channels of power, and unable to influence social and political change.

This restless quality is caught right from the opening Depression-era scene in which the beautiful but bored Bonnie (Faye Dunaway) sees the limping, toothpick-chewing, handsome Clyde (Warren Beatty) attempting to steal her mother's car and, caught up with his bravado, becomes involved in a life of crime. A life that takes them on a number of botched and bumbling robbery attempts, and after the addition of Clyde's crude, guffawing brother Buck (Gene Hackman), his bovine, pathetic wife Blanche (Estelle Parsons), and a nose-picking, hero-worshipping rustic driver named C. W. Moss (Michael Pollard), they go on a bank-robbing rampage that makes them celebrated and notorious figures.

Despite their violent and criminal acts, Penn never allows the audience's sympathy to leave Bonnie and Clyde. On the one hand, they are seen as outlaw-rebels (though never social victims) against an unjust social order of banks, police, and so on that brought on the Depression; on the other hand, they are innocent, awkward clowns (for example, Clyde is shocked when one of his victims tries to kill him with a cleaver). In addition, Penn attempts to reinforce our positive feelings for them, through his use of shallow Freudianism. Thus Clyde is sexually impotent, which supposedly provides the character with a measure of vulnerability, and gives his gun a crude, symbolic significance.

In depicting Bonnie and Clyde as ordinary folk, seeking to be immortalised, Penn sometimes catches the pathos underneath their posturing and bravado. For the slow, inarticulate Clyde and the slatternly, poetess manqué Bonnie – constantly looking at herself in a blurred mirror – are nothing more than a sharecropper and a waitress who hunger for the American dream of glamour and success. At the same time that Bonnie dresses in expensive clothes and obsesses about her image and making the headlines, she longs for home and mother. And though the scene where Bonnie returns to the family picnic is overly stylised and filled with soft-focused, sentimentalised, pastoral imagery (for example, a too picturesquely weathered and stark-looking farmwoman mother) it still succeeds in evoking a touch of the social world they came from.

However, what is most striking in the film is not their ordinariness or their psychological and social reality, but their mythic quality. It is a quality conveyed both by the glamour of stars like Beatty and Dunaway and by Penn's camera, which captures in long shot and close up the outlaws' vitality, spontaneity and style. In addition, their actions are framed by painterly, beautifully composed and melancholy images of sweeping wheat fields and prairies and Walker Evans-like small towns. It is all topped off by their slow-motion death, dressed in white (supposed innocence?), twitching like rag dolls in a montage of violence. Their death is both balletic and mythic, the tragic death of a heroic duo, and concrete, for the bullets are real and leave them truly dead. It is a sensual and exciting scene, but their death leaves one strangely unmoved.

The myth of Bonnie and Clyde works for Penn in aesthetic terms – the beauty of alienation and outlawry – and does capture something of how integral violence and the unfettered assertion of self and will was both to American mythology and to the sixties. It is when Penn wants his outlaws to be seen as romantic rebels against an unjust social order – Clyde returning money he stole to a poor farmer or the gang being embraced at a migrant camp (straight out of *The Grapes of Wrath*) as people's heroes – that the film becomes most simplistic and even dangerous. For it is clear that Penn wants Bonnie and Clyde to stand as symbols for the rebellious and high-spirited youth of the 1960s while the banks, Deputy Sheriff Homer and Pa Moss represent a cold, rigid and two-faced adult world. There are also suggestions, in the exaggerated, murderous use of police firepower (for example, a bloody shoot out where the police use an armoured car) of the American military's penchant for overkill in Vietnam.

However, no matter that Clyde talks about protecting poor

folk, their social consciousness never seems more than a contrivance of Penn's. The only community Bonnie and Clyde are members of is the criminal one, and though the film might not have had any more pernicious influence than getting somebody to buy a snap-brim hat, it did give symbolic sanction to certain nihilistic values and strains permanent in both the 'counter-culture' and the New Left, since it fed the contempt many of the young had for the adult world and its work ethic. And more significantly, by affirming criminality as a viable means of social, political and cultural protest, it fed the growing contempt that many of the young felt for more orthodox forms of political organisation and action, and ominously romanticised sociopathic violence by conceiving of and confusing it with acts of social rebellion.[32]

These objections aside, *Bonnie and Clyde* was still the landmark film of the sixties. Along with revitalising the formal dimensions of the Hollywood film, its focusing of attention on the young and the alienated gave some Hollywood lustre to the 1960s revisionist impulse which saw American history and society from the bottom up. Once launched on this road the easy shibboleths about America that had been Hollywood's stock in trade since the Second World War became harder and harder to sustain. And while many of these new notions were transformed into a kind of bankable and facile pessimism to go along with super-star directors and actors, they nevertheless did illuminate an America no longer as sure of itself and its values as had once been the case.

Nowhere is the crumbling of these values more clearly illustrated than in Mike Nichols' apotheosis of the young, *The Graduate* (1967), an extremely commercially successful film whose most compelling moment is the post-nuptial abduction of the beautiful Elaine Robinson (Katherine Ross) by the romantically obsessed Benjamin Braddock (Dustin Hoffman). Not only did this scene break with a whole genre past that upheld the sanctities of the marriage vow above everything, it was merely the ultimate and shrewdest (it gave Hollywood a breakthrough into the 18–25 market) assault in a whole series of attacks on the values of the affluent, upper-middle-class American.

The embodiment of this challenge in *The Graduate* is the

return of the bright and inexperienced Benjamin Braddock to the emptiness and sterility of his parent's Southern California world of swimming pools and economic security. Out of a sheer sense of ennui and alienation, Ben begins a sexually satisfying but emotionally starved affair with the bored, frustrated wife of his father's law partner, Mrs Robinson (Anne Bancroft). In contrast to the deadness of his affair with Mrs Robinson is the spontaneity and openness he finds with her daughter Elaine, despite her mother's violent objection to their relationship. Benjamin and Elaine share a commitment to see the world with honesty and clarity, to recognise both their loneliness and their estrangement from the parental world. And Nichols skilfully evokes empathy in the youth audience from Benjamin's truth-seeking and rejection of the plastic, unfeeling adult universe.

Combining the New Wave techniques of jump cuts, extreme close ups, and telephoto lens shots (throughout one senses Nichols' eclectic, stylistic borrowings from Antonioni, Fellini and Godard) with the music of the youth-culture heroes, Simon and Garfunkel, Mike Nichols was able to create a world of youth surrounded by stereotyped adults who were either predators or fools. Predictably, the gilded surfaces of the adults covered empty lives, dead marriages and emotionally wasted people all echoing, in the words of Simon and Garfunkel, the 'sounds of silence'.

In such a void the mere act of honestly being in love is seen as liberating and capable of shattering old verities, even the supposed eternal links of 'I do'. Therefore, Mrs Robinson's shriek at the runaway Elaine, that it's 'too late', can be met with the reply, 'not for me'. Nonetheless, this hardly guarantees a 'they live happily ever after' fade out; and the film ends with the couple's blank and ambiguous stares as they leave the scene of the wedding in the back of a municipal bus.[33]

Regardless of this final seed of doubt about the future, *The Graduate* still remains a hymn to the young. Like *Bonnie and Clyde* it grants all vitality, spontaneity and life to the young, adding to that list as well, all honesty, hope and idealism. However, in contrast to the origins of *Bonnie and Clyde*'s revolt, which was loosely and vaguely tied to the Depression, the reasons for Ben's alienation are projected into the sterility of a middle-class affluence. Taken together both films affirmed the discontent of the young, and in the case of *The Graduate* underlined that dissatisfaction by locating it precisely at the moment when the American dream seemed at its peak of material fulfilment, thus creating a paradigm for the type of sixties' film which attempted to subvert the values that had dominated American films since the 1940s. For not only was the language and sexual detail franker in *The Graduate*, but the insistence on a moral perspective which unambiguously repudiated social convention and taboos was relatively new to Hollywood. Indeed, with its oblique references to 1960s radicalism when its locale is shifted from Southern California to Berkeley (where a harried Benjamin follows Elaine) and a comic landlord who dislikes outside agitators is brought briefly into the film, *The Graduate* gave hints that there might be even more to Benjamin's anguish than alienation from the values of the upper-middle-class and existential angst. But *The Graduate* was based on a 1950s novel by Charles Webb and the film's few 1960s allusions did little to update the novel and truly illuminate the sources of student rebellion and alienation in the 1960s.

Needless to say, something about the intensity of *Bonnie and Clyde*'s violence and the extremity of Benjamin's alienation betokened something more public and political, something which made film-makers avert their eyes. That something was the war in Vietnam. Aware of the divided nature of American public opinion about the war, producers hesitated to tackle the subject directly. However, for a right-wing super-star and patriot like John Wayne, a film about the Vietnam war was a means of winning the hearts and minds of the American people.

Since the 1940s and films like *Wake Island* (1942), *They Were Expendable* and *Sands of Iwo Jima* (1949), John Wayne had become the symbol *par excellence* of the tough, efficient, patriotic American fighting man. The Wayne image was indelibly imprinted on every American schoolboy's imagination and every raw recruit's dreams. Nor was there anything ironic or calculating in Wayne's devotion himself to the image as exemplified by his red-baiting leadership in the McCarthyite Motion Picture Alliance for the Preservation of American Ideals, and his support of bellicose right-wing politicians like Barry Goldwater and Ronald Reagan.

Choosing as the subject of his Vietnam film the elite, military superhuman Green Berets, Wayne was in a sense returning to the world of his mentor, John Ford. Ford's cavalry units, perched at the edge of the frontier, were bastions of communal honour, tradition, camaraderie and pride, fighting an often little appreciated and less understood battle for civilisation and decency against the barbarians. Similarly, Wayne's Green Berets were a fortress of muscular and professional anti-communist values whose most serious challenge came ironically enough not from the communists, but from a liberal, sceptical reporter, George Beckwith (David Jannsen). However, his piddling doubts are suppressed as soon as Beckwith is exposed to the murderous brutality (they torture and rape) of a Vietcong (Indian) raid on a desolate and isolated Vietnamese village.

If the first half of the film is mediocre John Ford (the Vietcong are even seen scaling with ladders the Green Berets' Fort which is aptly named Dodge City), the second half is pure Richard Nixon. In this portion Wayne, using all manner of advanced technologies and tried and true dirty tricks (including a Mata Hari female decoy), kidnaps an enemy Vietcong general (whose aristocratic life style makes even his revolutionary politics suspect) from his secret headquarters. Through all of this Wayne hovers about like a good paterfamilias granting absolution to the liberal columnist for his political sins, and providing fatherly comfort to a cute Vietnamese orphan, who in Wayne's fadeout comment is 'What this is all about'.[34]

Although *The Green Berets* (1968) turned out to be financially profitable, rather than setting Americans' minds at ease about the righteousness of their cause it produced new evidence of the national split on the war. Indicative of that polarisation was some of the critical reaction to the film. In previous years a Wayne film rarely raised anything more than a critical ho-hum. However, the *Green Berets* provoked *New York Times* critic Renata Adler's withering comment that: '*The Green Berets* is a film so unspeakable, so stupid, so rotten and false that it passes through being funny, through being camp, through everything and becomes an invitation to grieve not so much for our soldiers or Vietnam (the film could not be more false or do greater disservice to them) but for what has happened to the fantasy-making apparatus of this country.'[35]

Adler's comment recognised that Hollywood's myth-making capacity had lost power and resonance and consequently the old Hollywood formulae could no longer capture and spur the nation's imagination to greater commitment in the war. No longer could Wayne's war-loving, patriarchal figure, spouting the old patriotic and macho certainties and clichés about decent, freedom-loving Americans and brutal, totalitarian Vietcong, capture and dominate the moral centre of the American imagination as it once had. Instead, Wayne's values existed in uneasy proximity to Hollywood's new revisionism featuring genre films that not only undermined Wayne's most cherished beliefs, but covertly and slyly evoked a Vietnam war with horror rather than honour as its prime component.

One such film was Sam Peckinpah's (a descendant of pioneers) brilliantly cut and richly composed and detailed western *The Wild Bunch* (1969). Paradoxically *The Wild Bunch* drew much of its power from working against the Fordian-Hawksian tradition that had done so much for Wayne's reputation. For instance, *The Wild Bunch* took place when the frontier was closed physically, and the ethos of the Old West disappearing fast in the wake of new technologies such as the motor car and the machine gun. Also fading with it were the elite band of mythic professional good-bad Robin Hoods that often populated the moral landscapes of Hawks and Ford. In contrast, in *The Wild Bunch* we have the almost interminable wranglings and whorings of Pike Bishop's (William Holden) gang of bank robbers and payroll snatchers, who are in turn pursued by a group of craven, rednecked, *lumpen* bounty hunters led by Pike's old confederate, the melancholy, trapped, Deke Thorton (Robert Ryan). In addition, the traditional Hollywood western town, which often manifested some communal pride, concern and virtue, has been replaced by a passive, foolish citizenry, too cowed and confused to make even more than a token protest when the streets of their town erupt with bloody, chaotic violence. The only active members of the town are its children, who mimic the shoot out and are demonically amused by burning to death the scorpions and ants they have been playing with.

With society corrupt and rapacious and the mythic west gone, the film follows Bishop's bunch becoming involved in the Mexican Revolution (whose politics Peckinpah cares nothing about) and in the process trying to establish some kind of rough set of principles. The value they place most importance on is that of group loyalty, the kind embodied in Bishop's comment that: 'When you side with a man, you side with him all the way – otherwise you're an animal'. Ultimately, this steadfastness grows among the outlaws and even comes to include the primal, savage Gorch Brothers (Ben Johnson and Warren Oates) and the Mexican bandit Angel (Jaime Sanchez). Almost as significant is the need to define some legitimate authority in a world of corrupt betrayers whose institutional power is dominated by debauchees like the gross, murderous Mexican general Mapache (Emilio Fernandez) and the ruthless railroad executive Harrigan (Albert Dekker). Something which makes it imperative, according to Dutch (Ernest Borgnine), Pike's Lieutenant, to weigh heavily the fact of not only just giving your word (the old code), but also: 'Who you give it to'.

However, whatever scrupulousness the outlaws exhibit toward their code is not matched by any restraint on Peckinpah's part in his depiction of violence in the film. For a supposed moralist, Peckinpah's use of graphic, elongated and sensational violence throughout the film – a horse stomping on a woman and dragging a man along the ground and countless bodies falling in slow motion with blood gushing from them – raised again questions about the origins and effects of screen violence. The answer this time was not only the usual talk about the psychology of the director and Hollywood's tendency to indulge in and exploit violence, but also a crediting of responsibility to the audience's increasing receptivity to violence, some of it caused by the nightly scenes of Vietnam bloodletting they saw on the television screen.

The climax of *The Wild Bunch*, with its stylised, orgiastic massacre, raised questions not only about the often incoherent blend of moralism and nihilism pervading Peckinpah's work, but also about the hopelessness reflected in many of the films of the late 1960s. Although *The Wild Bunch* ends on a supposedly revolutionary note with the last survivors both of the outlaws and of the bounty hunters, wise Old Sykes (Edmond O'Brien) and Deke Thornton, joining with the revolutionaries, the gesture seems an artificial afterthought following the more emotionally and aesthetically intense and compelling slaughter scenes. In fact, Peckinpah's deepest and most sentimental loyalties clearly have nothing to do with social commitment. It is men like Pike, seen in low-angle shots walking tall to a drum beat and resolving to die heroically, who elicit Peckinpah's deepest feeling. Pike and the men of the wild bunch may be brutal killers who belong to the past, but Peckinpah grants a final, heroic eulogy (shades of Ford's *Fort Apache*, 1948) as they are superimposed in their moment of transcendence over the film's concluding images – riding out of a Mexican village to the applause and serenades of its inhabitants.[36]

The *Wild Bunch*'s mixture of intellectual incoherence and weakness and imaginative and powerful imagery was symptomatic (though in exaggerated form) of the problems that many of these late sixties' films exhibited. The film-makers revelled in the freedom they now had to pursue previously forbidden subject matter and imagery, but were often incapable of doing more than evoking an image of a world gone awry. The directors were clearly more at home with images of human corruption, alienation, confusion and rebellion than with incisive and complex social and political critiques, and more attuned to feelings of anger and resentment towards and the desire for 'freedom' from conventional mores and established institutions than to any overviews of the malaise and movements of the sixties.

In films such as Arthur Penn's elegiac and loosely episodic *Alice's Restaurant* (1969) the prime purpose is to provide an evocation of the counter-culture. Using a ballad-like structure and centring the film around a solemn, honest, pure Arlo Guthrie (playing himself with consummate impassivity) the film touches on Arlo's relationship with the Old Left (via visits to his dying father, the legendary Woodie Guthrie); his conflicts with the establishment – college, police, army; and of course, the nature of the counter-culture, its inanities (a groupie offering to sleep with Arlo because someday he might 'become an album') and its luminous possibilities: a complex portrait of a commune presided over by Arlo's animated surrogate parents, the sensual, earth mother Alice Brock (Pat Quinn), and her insecure, hostile, dreamer husband Ray (James Broderick).

In *Alice's Restaurant* Penn's sympathies are clearly with the counter-culture as he wittily portrays Arlo's victories over the police (he beats a conviction for littering) and the draft. These scenes wryly and satirically capture the estrangement between the generations in America. Nonetheless, if Penn likes the young's openness and spontaneity he also understands that the counter-culture has flaws and sores of its own. For though Arlo can tranquily triumph over traditional institutions, another member of the commune, Shelley, dies of an overdose of heroin. More importantly, the image of the commune as a beatific refuge (they even reconsecrate an abandoned church), coexists with a profound sense of its futility and failure. The film concludes with a tortured Ray manically and desolately fantasising about creating one more commune, and with Penn's camera tenderly panning around Alice, who stands vulnerable and alone with both the commune and her marriage heading for disaster.

Alice's Restaurant is filled with luminous, poetic and painterly images, and has a real empathy for the counter-culture. Penn can grace us with beautiful moments, suggestions both of the absurdity and the sense of human possibility of the counter-culture; however, the film's structure is too loose and there are too many tones inhabiting the work – comic, pathetic and ironic – ultimately dissipating the emotional and intellectual impact of *Alice*. We also never get close enough to the Brocks or the commune to discover what truly caused their respective breakdowns.[37]

If *Alice's Restaurant*, in its inchoate way, does not always have control of its ambiguous portrait of the counter-culture, a film like the left-liberal *Medium Cool* (1969) often tends to sacrifice its politics for flashy cinematic effects. In *Medium Cool* the hero is a TV cameraman, John (Robert Forster), a detached, hard-boiled onlooker at contemporary events until he becomes emotionally and sexually involved with a reticent widow from Appalachia, Eileen (Verna Bloom), and her son (Harold Blankenship). Simultaneously, John also becomes politically conscious when he finds out that the FBI is being allowed to use his footage to identify radicals.

Medium Cool's director, Haskell Wexler, uses the fact that John is a TV cameraman to mix *cinéma vérité*-documentary and neo-documentary footage with his fictional narrative in order to create a relatively authentic portrait of sixties' social reality. And though there are scenes that take facile pot shots at easy targets, the film is filled with incisive sequences depicting angry black militants, insensitive white liberals, Illinois National Guardsmen receiving riot training, and the Chicago 1968 riots. However, the purely fictional scenes are much less convincing and are often left hanging as a couple of *vérité* scenes are inserted between them.

Medium Cool is an inconsistent work fluctuating between excessive and awkward Pirandello-like effects (the actors walk through the *vérité* scenes and the audience views Wexler and his crew shooting the final fatal accident scene), and telling images of the 1960s ethos. The final scene where John and Eileen die in a car crash ends the film on a dark, hopeless note – a climax which feels simultaneously gratuitous and contrived, and on another level conveys a sense of the fatality and destruction of the sixties.[38]

The most socially significant and commercially successful of these cinematic attempts at capturing the rebellious and alternate life styles of the 1960s was *Easy Rider* (1969). Initially conceived of as a kind of American International Pictures' exploitation quickie about the hippie scene like the *Wild Angels* (1966) and *The Trip* (1967), it had to be finished with independent financing by its star Peter Fonda. Its subsequent box office success compared to its initial investment would make it the model for what became known as the New American Cinema: independently financed, low-budget films, made by non-studio-trained directors, who combined highly personal or politically radical stories that broke with conventional Hollywood narrative techniques while borrowing heavily from the New Wave, *cinéma vérité*, and *avant-garde* films. Offshoots of this tendency were *Hi Mom* (1970), *Greetings* (1968), *Putney Swope* (1969), *Coming Apart* (1969), *Wild 90* (1968), *Ice* (1970), and other films of the late sixties and early seventies. Crucial to *Easy Rider*'s enormous commercial success and significance was its ability to capture on a visceral level certain prime themes and concepts of the counter-culture and the sixties – mysticism, freedom, 'the land', drugs and communes. It begins as a reverse road film in which a pair of hippie motorcyclists – the supercool, detached Wyatt (Peter Fonda) and the tense, angry and comic Billy (Dennis Hopper) – sell a kilo of dope to a Los Angeles hippie capitalist and then head east for Mardi Gras in what seems like a search for freedom. Along the way *Easy Rider* becomes a laid-back *bildungsroman* of America as the duo visit old-time ranchers and hippie communes, spend time in jail and in brothels, and take acid trips. The trip is enhanced by the film's exciting use of landscape, space, movement and sound (especially the contemporary rock music of Jimi Hendrix, the Byrds, Steppenwolf and others).

Unfortunately, the film was often painfully inarticulate, shallow and pretentious when it tried to deal with ideas. Most of these took the form of particularly banal and sententious pronouncements by the hippie saint Wyatt, who gives a benediction to the commune ('They're gonna make it'), or pays pious reverence to the life style of a toothless old rancher ('doing his own thing, in his own time').

However, in its depiction of Us against Them, the free, long hairs versus the vicious, redneck straights, the film did strike a powerful social and emotional chord. Moreover, in the process it gave up its penchant for indulging in ersatz and sentimental beatitudes, and connected to the disillusionment felt by many (especially the young) about the America of the sixties. Its most poignant expression came in the comment of an articulate, amiable, alcoholic lawyer, George Hanson (Jack Nicholson), who joins the two on their quest, and after being attacked by local goons makes the point that: 'This used to be a helluva country. I can't understand what's going on'.

Hanson's remark sets the tone of the second half of the film, which is pervaded with as much of a sense of doom, failure and despair as the opening was with space, light and movement. Indeed, Wyatt's and Billy's own violent fate is prefigured in George's murder by a group of rednecks. And although they do make it to the Mardi Gras, and take an extravagantly filmed acid trip (fisheye lens, overexposed images, and overlapping dialogue) with some prostitutes in a cemetery, their pathetic destiny seems so sealed that we get hints of it in flashforwards and Wyatt's final pronouncement that 'We Blew It'. It is a climax that not only acted as a judgment on their personal quest, but seemed to extend to the American experience as a whole.

Such was the outrage of some critics at this judgment, that an elite, cultural custodian like Diana Trilling (who had not raised more than an eyebrow at films since her tenure as a reviewer for the *New Republic* in the forties and fifties) was moved to call the film 'devious'. She was also particularly peeved by the use and appropriateness of Wyatt and Billy as symbols of our social and cultural condition and complained that: 'Wyatt and Billy lack the energy to create anything, comment on anything, feel anything, except the mute, often pot-induced pleasure of each other's company'.[39]

However, though one may quarrel with the presumptious-ness of having two dope-dealing drifters both stand as symbols of freedom and make judgments on something as vast as the 'American experience', there is little doubt that *Easy Rider* captured that sense of foreboding and doom which dominated many of the films of the sixties, and heralded those of the seventies. In fact, the fate of Wyatt and Billy seemed a reflection of what had been the fate of Martin Luther King, Malcolm X and Robert Kennedy, and some felt could be the lot of anyone whose dissent and protest truly threatened the power structure in America.

Of course, Billy and Wyatt were far from being political protesters or reformers, but in their dim, self-destructive way they were searching for some vague alternative to the dominant culture. *Easy Rider* is an inarticulate film which succeeds in evoking the mood of a decade, and in its mixture of intellectual simple-mindedness, striking imagery and editing, and conscious and unconscious intuition into the decade's confusion and alienation, it was one of the most representative of late 1960s films. In fact, Wyatt's despairing comment grants unintentional pop-cultural symmetry to a decade which began with the unequivocal optimism embodied in lyrics of songs like 'Blowin' in the Wind' and ended with the pessimism of a line like 'We Blew It'.

5.   The Seventies

On 18 March 1969, newly elected President Richard Nixon ordered the bombing of Cambodia. It was the first in a series of events whose consequences were to dominate American politics and society during the first half of the seventies. Given Nixon's past history – his hawkish foreign policy views and his gift for manipulating anti-communism to further his political career – there should have been little surprise that he ordered the bombing. However, in 1968 Nixon had come to power primarily on the strength of his vague promise that he knew how to end the war, and here he was extending the war into a neutral country and compounding his actions by taking it in the strictest secrecy. For Nixon knew that at this point in the Vietnam war neither Congress nor the public would have approved of its escalation.[1]

Needless to say, Richard Nixon and his advisers were hardly conscious of the irony inherent in their actions. They had dropped the Johnson–Humphrey beliefs about the war being fought for ideals like 'democracy' or 'self-determination', and had little use even for geopolitical rationales like the fear of toppling Southeast Asian dominoes. Their rationale for continuing US involvement in Vietnam was summed up by the strategic concept of 'credibility'. They believed that the war had to be fought to maintain America's reputation 'as a guarantor' – to assure her allies (and more particularly her enemies) that the US would be firm in confronting a crisis.[2]

Inextricably connected to the idea of 'credibility' was the notion of 'American Will'. The world had to be assured that America would take the necessary painful steps, like the bombing of Cambodia, to back up words with action. After the American people finally became aware of the bombing the

President told them, 'it is not our power but our will and character that is being tested tonight'.[3]

To the Nixon administration that will seemed badly shaken after years of seemingly interminable bloodshed, the investment of billions of dollars and the often violent debate and struggle that had produced a divided nation. To some in the administration there was even a suspicion that the will had been permanently damaged not only by the war, but by social welfarism, government intervention in the economy, and the leadership of a decadent elite and establishment.

In order to renew this will, Richard Nixon set about attacking the media, liberal-left intellectuals and government bureaucrats – institutions which he perceived as establishment bastions. It was a campaign motivated almost as much by Nixon's own sense of powerlessness and private grievance as by ideological and political commitments. In initiating this attack Nixon dismantled much of the 'Great Society' legislation of the Johnson presidency, stacked the Supreme Court with judicial conservatives, and attempted the political mobilisation of a segment of the American population he dubbed the 'silent majority' (supposedly ordinary Americans who adhered to traditional verities like patriotism) in opposition to both the 'establishment' and the war protesters.

Given that Nixon's policies were dependent on smears, innuendo, confrontation and polarisation, they succeeded only in fragmenting any semblance of an American will. They pitted race against race, old against young, class against class, and region against region, leaving division rather than unity in their wake. However, this further disruption of the American will did not contradict the goals of the Nixon administration, for what Nixon and his associates were really interested in creating was not a harmonious and cohesive American society and spirit, but an administration which embodied and defined the national will. It was this confidence (megalomania?) that his administration really was an expression of the American will which provided Nixon with the rationale to indulge in whatever he felt politically necessary: to concentrate power in the White House; to use war methods against domestic enemies; and to use the power of the federal government to promote and maintain the image and reputation of the administration. In fact for Nixon and his cohorts the image the administration projected was more significant than the substance, a notion which was far from new to American politics, but clearly gained much strength during the 1970s.[4]

In promoting their image the Nixon administration initiated a campaign of illegal activities. In 1971, after the release of the Pentagon Papers, they created a group of undercover operatives nicknamed 'the plumbers'. It was the covert activities of this group which led to the break-in at Democratic headquarters in June 1972 and the resulting Watergate scandal. The public revelation of the scandal and the administration's cover-up led to the resignation of Nixon – though even in his final days of power Nixon was unable to confront and admit his own responsibility in the whole affair. The forcing out of office of Nixon and his hatchet man, Vice President Agnew (for bribe-taking), undermined both the institution of the Presidency and the whole American political ethos. The public began to distance itself from politics, expressing only cynicism about the rhetoric and programmes that politicians proposed. By 1973 it was clear that the political passions and polarisation of the sixties had died, to be replaced by a general sense of alienation and apathy.[5]

Paralleling that shift in the public mood was the replacement of Nixon by his appointed Vice President Gerald Ford, the perfect figure to preside over a period of political stagnation. In 1976 Ford led a Bicentennial celebration of American independence. The frenetic activity and the overblown rhetoric were a self-conscious attempt by Americans to demonstrate their confidence in the country despite almost fifteen years of wars, recessions, riots, and the assassinations and resignations of its leaders. The most poignant expression of this need for self-congratulation occurred in New York City. In 1975, perhaps symbolic of American society and especially of its older urban areas, New York had been brought to the brink of bankruptcy by a combination of such factors as middle-class flight, rising crime, a reduced tax base, increased demands for public services from a growing poverty population, economic demands of municipal unions and the callousness and rapacity of the city's major banks. Only a last-minute loan guarantee by the federal government staved off financial catastrophe.

However, despite, or more likely because of, these economic and social conditions, New York staged 'Operation Sail', one of the most impressive of the Bicentennial ceremonies. During this celebration a fleet of white-sailed schooners and frigates from all over the world sailed up and down the Hudson River to the applause of immense crowds. New York's elaborate ceremony seemed to embody the nation's desire to affirm the power and resilience of the American will – no matter what the concrete realities were like.[6]

In fact, Jimmy Carter based his campaign for the Democratic Presidential nomination in 1976 on just this national need to renew its belief in itself. Carter, a man of deep religious convictions (he was a 'born again Christian') was aware of the country's need for spiritual talk rather than political rhetoric and programmes. In his standard speech he talked about a government as good as its people, implicitly affirming a belief that the American will and spirit were still strong and vital. He also shrewdly sensed that after Nixon, the 'character issue' was a prime one for the American public, and he promised in Sunday School terms never to lie to the people.

In addition, Carter benefited from other American social and political strains. A 'New South' had emerged since the 1960s, for with de jure elimination of racial segregation, Carter no longer had to deal with the Southern politician's albatross of the Civil War, Reconstruction and Jim Crow. Secondly, Carter was not a national politician or party chieftain, he was an outsider (one term Governor of Georgia) who could be projected as a fresh face untainted by Watergate. Finally, the all-pervasive power of the media had made it possible for a political figure to jump from obscurity to celebrity merely by making a number of successful television appearances.[7]

Carter's campaign avoided dealing with the issues or taking hard positions, and by invoking moral pieties and capitalising on his outsider status he won a narrow victory over Ford in the 1976 election. However, though he was a skilled diagnostician of the public's yearning, Carter's political talents did not seem to extend beyond the pursuit of power and the winning of elections. His first year in office was committed more to symbolism than to substance. Informal state dinners, telephone talks with ordinary citizens and spending the night at their homes, and wearing a cardigan sweater while announcing an energy plan which he conceived as the moral equivalent of war did not help him with Congress. Carter confronted an assertive Congress which after Vietnam and Watergate was profoundly wary of the executive branch. Furthermore, Carter carried over from his campaign a blurriness over issues and an inability to make hard decisions. He equivocated in the Bert Lance scandal, tarnishing his image for integrity, and seemed to lack control over his cabinet and his low-comic brother Billy. More and more there existed a growing feeling that Jimmy Carter was too small a man to handle the Presidency.[8]

In July 1979, after repeated attempts to untangle his administration, Carter tried to liberate himself from his ineffective and incompetent image by firing a number of cabinet members (Califano, Blumenthal *et al.*) and making a speech updating his energy policy. It was more than just a speech about energy, it was in typical Carter style an expression of moral concern which attempted to rouse the American people from their malaise. It was a call to strengthen the American will by ridding it of its self-indulgence: 'The erosion of our confidence in the future is threatening to destroy the social and political fabric of America . . . we have learned that piling-up material goods cannot fill the emptiness of lives which have no confidence or purpose.'[9]

Though this ministerial oratory was no substitute for a coherent energy policy, Carter's rhetoric did have cultural resonance and significance for the seventies. It paralleled the writing of culture critics such as Christopher Lasch and Tom Wolfe, who had dubbed the 1970s a narcissistic era, a 'me decade'. They perceived the age as a time when people were intent on polishing, cultivating and doting upon themselves and their relationships without regard to politics, society or posterity. The seventies had produced a culture built on a cult of personal relations which was often simply an expression and a result of a chaotic and destructive social order and devastated and empty private lives. The culture craved intimacy without genuine human connection or sacrifice, material plenty without productivity, and success without real content or accomplishment. Hedonistic consumerism and the ethic of self-preservation had become the order of the day.[10]

To some extent this collective narcissism was partially brought on by the failure and collapse of the New Left and counter-culture in the early seventies. The 'Movement' (differing from the old left) was concerned with problems of personal identity and authenticity. However, these problems (especially for those who were political or social activists) were rarely separated from their commitment to transforming American society. Of course, there were others who treated social activism as merely a substitute for personal therapy. But by the seventies many of the survivors of the 'Movement' had decided that one of the reasons for its failure (neglecting or dismissing historical and political explanations) was the nature of political commitment itself. That what was now necessary to achieve some sense of peace and fulfilment was getting directly to the bottom of the self through various self-awareness movements (Est and Arica), oriental gurus and bioenergetics.[11]

The interesting fact about this intense preoccupation with the self and its needs was that it assumed that unlimited personal growth would coincide with unlimited material prosperity. This belief was based on the post-Second World War notion that continuous expansion was inherent in the very nature of the American economy, and though blatant racial and economic inequities existed in America in the years from 1945 through the early seventies, the Americans had the resources to create an economy successful enough to satisfy the material needs and yearnings of the majority of the people. Within that expansionist framework, American capitalism could vitiate resentment by keeping unemployment low, increasing social services and mediating between the interests of capital and labour.

However, in the mid-1970s a change in public consciousness occurred. For the first time in American history public opinion polls reported that the American people were no longer optimistic about the nation's future. The country was beset with an economic crisis, which in fact was an underlying cause of Carter's 1976 victory. But Carter was ultimately unable to turn the economy around. By the end of his term rising oil prices, a debt-laden balance of payments and the lack of competitiveness of the motor and steel industries had again thrown the American economy into severe recession.

Consequently in the 1980 election Carter was soundly defeated and the ex-actor and California governor, Ronald Reagan, was elected by a landslide to the Presidency. There were many reasons for the repudiation of Carter and the Democrats, a recoil from big government and liberalism (though Carter was no liberal), personal rage and resentment towards Carter's supposed weakness and incompetence, and most importantly the hope that Reagan would resurrect the American will from its malaise. The public craved a candidate untouched by a sense of complexity and ambiguity, who could successfully package a simple belief in American might, power and opportunity to right the ills of the nation. However, in 1980 the rebirth of the American will existed only in the realm of political rhetoric, the country was beset with perilous economic, social and international difficulties which clearly would not be resolved by the intoning of patriotic and moralistic platitudes.[12]

During the seventies the film industry and its product reflected the confusion and malaise permeating the American will. At the beginning of the decade the industry was a chronic invalid, with studios losing a combined aggregate of $500 million dollars between 1969 and 1972, only to renew itself financially during the second half of the decade with grosses of almost 3 billion dollars. Early in the decade the old studios connected their fortunes to those of huge conglomerates like Kinney National Service. As a result, the men who produced the films had their eyes glued to the balance sheets rather than to the rushes. That meant fewer pictures, but those that were made had generous publicity budgets geared primarily to a youth audience between the ages of 12 and 26.

Another element in this process was the changing relationship between the cinema and TV. It began with a period of all-out-war in the fifties, moved to the casual embrace of the sixties, and by the seventies the film industry's relationship with television had become a passionate one; by pre-selling their films both to pay and commercial television and cashing in on new video software (cassettes, discs and so on) the possibility of Hollywood losing immense sums of money on films had become slight. No longer did a studio have to worry about possible bankruptcy if one heavily financed film failed.[13]

There was at least one beneficial result from the financial difficulties of the seventies. In groping around for any means to make a comeback, the studios began to take chances and reach out to relatively untried film-makers such as Robert Altman, Martin Scorsese, Brian de Palma, Peter Bogdanovitch, Steven Spielberg, Michael Ritchie and Francis Ford Coppola.[14]

What distinguished these directors was their awareness of film history, technical competence (sometimes gained from working on small-budget quickies or in university film schools) and self-conscious personal visions. For instance Robert Altman directed films which were idiosyncratic versions of popular genres like *The Long Goodbye* (1973), engaged in social comment and satire in *Nashville* (1975), and made highly personal, dreamlike films like *Three Women* (1977). Brian de Palma's varied output included the Hitchcockian *Obsession* (1976) and the anarchic *Hi Mom* (1969) and *Greetings* (1968), and Francis Ford Coppola transformed the gangster film (*Godfather I* and *II*) into a tragic epic about Americanisation.

In stark contrast to the old studio days when these directors, their methods and themes and they themselves would have been subordinated to a whole battery of executive producers, they now retained a great deal more control over scripts and actors, and often even had the power of the final cut. The studios had become primarily financiers and distributors, treating film more as a business than an industry, and consequently taking more interest in profit margins than in the substance of their product.

The transformation of the studios and the success of this more personal form of film-making did not mean that Hollywood had opted for dispensing with the traditional genres. Genre films with their well-defined characters, actions and iconography still resonated with American audiences. In the sixties a number of films (for example, *Easy Rider*) both cut across and modified the traditional genres focusing on buddies (rather than Hollywood's usual solitary hero), the counter-culture and blacks. However, despite *Easy Rider* becoming (because of its low budget and personal style) a landmark for the directors of the seventies, these new genres did not sustain their audience appeal. A number of the seventies' directors did make films which turned back to conventional genres like the gangster film and the thriller, but the effects of the counter-culture and the New Left of the sixties and the sense of alienation and *anomie* were too great to make films which adhered to the structure and rules of classics like *The Big Sleep* (1946) and *Little Caesar* (1930). The genre conventions often existed now as a springboard for social commentary, psychological revelation or parody and satire.[15]

The best example of this use of genre was the protean Francis Ford Coppola's *The Godfather* (1972) and *The Godfather II* (1974). In their emphasis on the murders, violence and Machiavellian manipulations of criminals, these films indirectly reflected American involvement in Vietnam and the political crimes of Watergate. The films also echoed Balzac's famous comment that behind every great fortune there rested a crime. But beyond these images of American corruption, the two films used a driving narrative rhythm, a luxurious use of light and shadow, and almost voluptuous camera movements to evoke the destruction of the American Dream.

Coppola had the good fortune to base the films on a commercially successful pulp novel by Mario Puzo. What he and Puzo did was to invert the tradition of the gangster film. As Robert Warshow once wrote of the gangster film: 'Since we do not see the rational and routine aspects of the gangster's behavior, the practice of brutality – unmixed criminality – becomes the totality of his career'.[16] In *The Godfather* films Coppola begins with the very rituals and emotions that have been left out of the traditional gangster film – baptism and marriage, family solidarity and love – all of which serve as the foreground for criminality, violence and murder.

The *Godfather I* centred around these ceremonies and the very notion of family itself. Dominating the film is Don Vito Corleone (Marlon Brando), an almost mythological figure – a murderer who is totally at ease with his authority and power. He is a man whose prime goal is to keep his family from dancing to another's strings, who is committed to his family's security, dignity and independence. Don Vito is a powerful force who can absolve people of their guilt and protect them from hurt; he is a monster, but in Coppola's view an almost sacred one. In *The Godfather*, for every dark, shuttered room where business and murder are plotted, there are still scenes where children play, marriages are held and family and communal warmth and light exist. In fact, the Don is allowed to die peacefully, fondling his grandson among the tomato plants.

Some of *The Godfather*'s audience appeal must have derived from the sense of order it evoked. For in a time when many Americans felt the world had gone mad – when assassinations, war, corrupt politics and economic recession dominated the national landscape – there was a longing for a sane place where experience was relatively well-ordered and secure. In a film such as *American Graffiti* (1973) that time of innocence was placed in the fifties, and in *The Godfather* that haven was the ethnic family. However, *The Godfather* was a film drenched in blood and neither the depiction of strong family roots nor the Don's rough, natural sense of justice could cancel out the image of a family whose business and success were totally involved in murder.[17]

In *Godfather II*, Coppola decided to pursue the underside of the American success ethic in much greater depth. Using Don Vito's son and heir, Michael (Al Pacino) as the central character, the film captures the transformation of the American dream into a nightmare of alienation and dissolution. In *Godfather II* the old tribal Mafia of Don Vito's New York-based Genco Olive Oil Company with its numbers, juke boxes and prostitutes has begun to transform itself into a Lake Tahoe-based, acculturated, depersonalised, multi-national corporation. And with the abandonment of the old traditions, the quest both for legitimacy and for a veneer of corporate respectability has only tragic consequences.

Michael and 'the family' have made it in America, and are powerful enough to command the support of a hypocritical and venal US Senator, and to gather with the heads of other ('legitimate?') multi-national corporations to divide up the spoils in pre-Castro Havana. However, their mobility has brought neither happiness nor repose, just pain and fragmentation. Michael is sombre, remote and unfeeling, all his life energies projected into the 'business'. As a result of his talent for 'business', Michael is hated by his sister Connie (Talia Shire), betrayed by his ineffectual brother, Fredo (John Cazale) and estranged from his WASP wife Kay (Diane Keaton).

The decline of the family is filmed in dark, dimly-lit interiors and in sterile, luxurious rooms, where people can often be seen only in silhouette. It is a joyless world, and by intercutting and counterpointing luminous flashback sequences of the life of the young Don Vito (Robert DeNiro), Coppola succeeds in vividly heightening the bleakness and desolation of Michael's universe. For though the immigrant world of Don Vito's Little Italy may be impoverished and murderous, it is enveloped in golden-toned colours and light and shot in soft focus, nostalgically evoking a world of energy, warmth and community, and Don Vito himself is depicted in a heroic mould, an urban Robin Hood – courtly, self-possessed and courageous – a man who can redress the rapacity of exploitative landlords and is viewed with respect by his fellow immigrants. Coppola clearly does not hide the fact Don Vito is a criminal, but he is one whose profound familial feelings and natural grace make his criminality almost acceptable.

However, in the move from the world of tenements, push-carts and religious processions to the armed fortress in Lake Tahoe, the personal and the familial have been lost. The haven of the family and the ethnic community (however claustrophobic and destructive) cannot be sustained under the fragmenting pressures of the capitalist success ethic. Michael still tries to hold on to aspects of the code – he believes in machismo and the sacredness of the family – but they exist for him primarily as abstract and formal ideals, and he is never able to convey the love for his children which the young and old Don Vito radiate and bask in. In fact, it is Fredo who acts as surrogate father for Michael's unhappy, melancholy son, Anthony. By the end of the film the unforgiving Michael has murdered and lost almost everything he has cared for, and he can be seen in close up sitting in tragic isolation, his face turned into a ghostly death mask.

The *Godfather* films did not pretend to be or attempt to provide a sophisticated left critique of the institutional structure of capitalism. However, while operating within a commercial form they were able to convey the perniciousness of American capitalism. The films were an epic of dissolution: evoking how Americanisation and success turned murderous passion and loyalty into an impersonal, rootless nightmare.

And it is a nightmare which extends far beyond the parochial confines of the Mafia into the nature of American history and society itself.[18]

Another film which in a similar fashion was unconsciously and consciously influenced by the political and cultural ferment of the sixties was Robert Altman's *Nashville* (1975). The film was Altman's attempt at capturing middle-American consciousness, and the perniciousness and energy of America's popular culture which both shapes and expresses it.

Indicative of the film's importance was that the *New York Times* assigned Associate Editor Tom Wicker to write a think piece about it. In it he called *Nashville*: 'a two and half hour cascade of minutely detailed vulgarity, greed, deceit, cruelty, barely contained hysteria and the frantic lack of root and grace into which American life has been driven by its own heedless vitality.'[19]

In *Nashville* Altman interweaves twenty-four characters who are participants in or who dream of entering the world of country and western music. Using an open-ended and improvisational style, filled with dazzling aural and visual images, Altman evokes a callous, grasping, violent world in which everyone gropes for the main chance or survives on its leavings. The country and western stars are manipulative, absurd, hysterical: in the main, empty, vain people obsessed by crowd applause and their own status, while their public's behaviour ranges from breathless adulation to barbaric rage.

Among Altman's 'Grand Hotel' of stars is the doyen of country western music, Haven Hamilton (Henry Gibson), a diminutive, narcissistic and controlling figure stuffed into a tailored, sequined cowboy suit with a slightly askew toupee. Hamilton is a tough, vital and pompous little rooster whose songs, 'We Must Be Doing Something Right' and 'For the Sake of The Children', embody the soporific and saccharine values of Nashville. The singing star, Barbara Jean (Ronee Blakley), a madonna dressed in white, is a child-like, hysterical and neurasthenic figure. For Altman she is the prime symbol of how media creation and success victimise and destroy, and she exemplifies the agony and self-deception that lie between manufactured public roles and a fragile private existence.

Altman's other characters run the range from a handsome,

totally egoistical, stud rock singer who plays tapes of his songs while he sleeps, to a pathetic off-key singing waitress, a stiff, token 'white nigger singer', and a ridiculous and pretentious BBC journalist. They inhabit a world where relationships are subordinated to hustling for the main chance or to promiscuous scoring. It is a fragmented and alienated world, and Altman succeeds in making Nashville a metaphor for American life; a chaotic din where everybody is struggling for their own gold record.

In *Nashville* everything is packaged and mechanised, including politics. From the opening frame, when the sound track of the Replacement Party's presidential candidate, the pseudo-populist Hal Phillip Walker, patrols the pre-dawn empty streets, to the final shot of his limousine leaving the climactic assassination scene, politics play a significant role in the film. It is a politics built on a canned voice and an invisible candidate (we never see Walker, just the detached, contemptuous advance man, Triplette). And the party, with its slogan 'new roots for the nation' and platform calling for a new national anthem and the removal of lawyers from Congress, seeks national moral renewal by selling nostalgia and bumptious iconoclasm. The party is one more image without substance: boosters, and a sound truck hawking the vagaries of the platform in the same way as the record albums are hyped over the opening credits.

Altman has created, through dynamic and seamless cutting and unrelenting movement within the frame, a frenzied world. One thinks of Whitman's catalogues of America now gone amuck; sound tracks overlap, and cars crash, planes roar, marching bands perform and TV newsmen drone on. This grasping, frenetic world has its apotheosis in the assassination of Barbara Jean at a benefit concert for the Replacement Party in Nashville's Parthenon. In this powerful set piece of a finale, a seemingly innocuous boy with a guitar, possibly out of some oedipal rage or merely acting out the violence that permeates every pore of the society, shoots Barbara Jean. The act is an echo of the Oswalds, Sirhan Sirhan and Arthur Bremers – the assassins and psychopaths that wander and menace the streets of contemporary America.

In the aftermath the crowd, stunned and milling about,

begins to participate in the ironic and chillingly repeated lyric, 'You may say I ain't free, but it don't worry me'. What sounds like a stirring song of solidarity and the courage to go on is one more turn of the screw, accentuated by the fact that a black choir sings it. The camera pans to close ups of people in the crowd giving voice to the words and then zooms away to a long shot of the stupefied, acquiescent mass. The song is a hymn to apathy and accommodation, a metaphor for an America which accepts its bondage to the media's plasticity, artifice and banality.

Although this image of a friendly facism emerging from the popular culture to lure and seduce the people is powerful, it is too facile to be intellectually credible. Though pop music is used to manipulate and exploit, it still often has authentic folk roots, and can at moments (however ephemeral and superficial) generate a generational sense of solidarity and rebellion – witness the sixties. Altman also exaggerates popular culture's role as a prime agent of oppression. Indeed, it usually functions more as a reflection than as a real determinant of our deepest social and cultural tendencies. Of course, Altman is a director who is in love with surfaces, textures and images and has little interest in what lies beyond them. He never cares to examine popular music's historical and cultural content or the power groups that help shape the music industry, for Altman's ultimate commitment is to observation rather than exposition.

Nevertheless, if Altman's film is not a profound work of social criticism, it still hit on a raw nerve. In *Nashville* Altman intuitively understands how bountiful and destructive American popular culture is, and how the world of appearances often beguiles and rules Americans. Also, at the moments his suggestive metaphors and images come alive they conjure up a monstrous and irrational America which is much more vivid and resonant (and even truer) than the one constructed by more coherent and analytic critics.

Even if Altman may have placed too much stress on the media's ultimate power there was no gainsaying its effect on American society during the late sixties and seventies. For example, without television the anti-war and women's movements probably would not have had the same impact. Television covered feminist sit-ins at leading women's magazines and mass marches and demonstrations, and held discussions and debates on the changing roles and identities of men and women. Of course, they vulgarised and merchandised feminism in various sitcoms and commercials such as the one for Virginia Slims cigarettes.[20]

Television's attitude towards women and feminism was at best ambivalent and at worst thoroughly destructive, but it succeeded in forcing the movement into the consciousness of the American public. Without having a journalistic function, Hollywood in turn had even more difficulty in dealing with the women's issue, especially since it went deeper than just equal rights and equal pay and challenged sacred industry canons on sexuality and the family. For a time Hollywood seemed to have banished most women from the screen and replaced them with buddy films such as *Scarecrow* (1973), *Little Fauss and Big Halsey* (1970) and *The Sting* (1973), works which almost eliminated women from major roles and concentrated on macho exploits and homoerotic bonds.

However, at the same time, prodded by the women's movement and by powerful and popular female actresses such as Barbara Streisand and Jane Fonda, plus the rise of an independent women's cinema which produced films like *Joyce at 34* (1973), *Nana, Mom and Me* (1974) and *Union Maids* (1976), the film industry did take a few stabs at making films about women. One of the first of these, *Klute* (1971), was not only a box office success but an Academy award-winner as well.[21]

Klute is John Klute (Donald Sutherland) a strong, silent, small-town policeman who comes to New York to pursue leads in the disappearance and possible murder of a close friend. The film is stylishly directed by Alan Pakula (*All the President's Men*, 1976), creating a paranoid world of wiretaps and lurking silhouetted figures. Pakula's compositions are nervous with his characters often placed on the extreme edge of the frame, and he often blacks out part of the screen to create feelings of isolation and tension. But the real focus of the film is not urban paranoia or the sadistic violence that lies behind respectable, corporate facades; it is the struggle for self-definition of a prime suspect in the case, the prostitute, Bree Daniels (Jane Fonda).

Bree is a witty, seemingly confident, cynical and self-destructive woman who wants to control her life, but can only maintain it in the role of call girl. It is a life she knows is going nowhere. Nevertheless, as she tells her therapist about her tricks: 'I'm in control. When they come to me they're nervous, I'm not. I know what I'm doing. I know I'm good.' In contrast to her power over the Johns who share her bed, she has little control over the rest of her life. Although able to simulate sexual excitement and manipulate male fantasies as a prostitute, she is merely an object or image, a commodity to be dismissed when she pursues her acting and modelling careers.

What little control Bree has in her life is increasingly threatened by her love for Klute, an emotion she tries to fend off by continually manipulating and hurting him. Some of the film's best moments take place during Bree's sessions with her therapist, where she describes how she tries to destroy her feelings for Klute for fear they will engulf her. It is one of the few times in film that a therapeutic session seems natural and irreducible to psychological clichés and magical resolution.

Unfortunately, Klute's character does not quite transcend Hollywood stereotypes. He is portrayed as a man whose self-sufficiency is merely a muted affirmation of traditional Hollywood rites of machismo, and whose passivity is a form of aggression. But with the character of Bree the film grants us a sense of the problems of the seventies' 'new woman'. The breaking away from the old roles of female dependency and commitment to domesticity and family implies all sorts of new and anxiety-laden relationships and situations. At the end of the film Bree gives up her compulsive need to manipulate and control, and leaves with Klute for his hometown, but she is still ambivalent about the relationship and informs her therapist in a voiceover: 'I may be back in a couple of weeks'.[22]

While Bree does not make the complete break with the traditional women's role in Hollywood – she *may* be going off to live happily ever after – the film does give a feeling of a woman's struggle for a new identity and role. In a faltering manner, the film industry made a number of gestures towards confronting the social and psychological issues raised by the women's movement. Films such as *Blume in Love* (1973) and Martin Scorsese's *Alice Doesn't Live Here Anymore* (1974)[23] reflected, in a compromised and commercialised fashion, the industry's struggle with constructing an image of the 'new woman'. Some of the women's films made during the second half of the decade tended to trivialise the problem by tying it to outworn genres like the 'weepie' (*The Turning Point*, 1978) or a literate, female version of the buddy film (*Julia*, 1977). There were also films which claimed to be about liberated women, such as *The Unmarried Women* (1978) and *Kramer vs. Kramer* (1979) which either provided Prince Charmings to ease the pain of 'liberation' or criticised the callousness of the newly emancipated women.

Kramer vs. Kramer was 1979's biggest commercial and critical hit, winning five Oscars (including Best Film, Director and Actor) and grossing over 60 million dollars domestically. It was the kind of work that *Time* could tout as a minefield of contemporary social issues, and though it did indeed deal with the breakdown of traditional concepts of marriage and family and with the male assuming the maternal role, much of its massive success rested with its remaining human and cosy in the old Hollywood style. It is a film which keeps under control the despair and chaos inherent in the abandonment by the liberated wife-mother Joanna (Meryl Streep) of her husband Ted (Dustin Hoffman) and her son emphasising instead the growing warmth and love between father and son. It also comforts rather than disturbs the audience, assuring them that in a time of fragmentation where egoism is constantly celebrated, virtues such as loyalty, decency, and self-sacrifice still exist.

Kramer vs. Kramer is an intelligent and accessible work which succeeds in conveying fresh and unsentimental truths about parents and children; the relationship between father and son is evoked in all its anguish, pleasure and complication. The intensity of the father's love is most powerfully communicated in a scene where the boy receives a severe cut by falling off some playground monkey bars. The camera then focuses on Ted's despairing and guilt-ridden face as he races wildly with his son in his arms to the hospital. There are also perceptive scenes where Ted not only must try to be patient and compassionate with his son, but must feign affection and interest when he does not feel it or has his mind on other matters. And though Ted is clearly depicted as a caring, devoted father, he is also seen to be a prickly, tense and easily irritated man.

Nevertheless, *Kramer vs. Kramer*'s intelligence is repressed in a work which takes few formal or intellectual risks, a film whose emotions and images never suggest that there are levels of feeling and meaning that exist beyond what appears on the surface. Also there is a strain of anti-feminism here. It is Ted who garners the film's sympathy and applause by displaying the humanness and emotional strength (not without difficulty) to be both capable of pursuing a career and being a nurturing, committed parent. The wife's consciousness is never explored (except for the opening moments where in desperation and sorrow she prepares to tell her husband that she is leaving), and she is given lines that do not elicit sympathy and are relentlessly packaged feminist clichés: anguished-women-submerged-by-domesticity-careerist-husband-in-search-of-self.[24]

Nevertheless, despite these profound limitations there have clearly been advances for women in the films of the 1970s. Women's issues have been consciously foregrounded and built into the narrative of the films, in ways the Katherine Hepburn and Bette Davis films rarely did. But by the end of most of these films the women are usually back in place next to their man, despite the struggles they have put up through the body of the work.

In sharp contrast to the increasing number of women's films was the disappearance of serious films about black life (almost as if echoing the Nixon–Moynihan notion of 'benign neglect'). Black films had been commercially successful in the early seventies, movies like *Shaft* (1971) and *Superfly* (1972) ushered in a whole new genre called blaxploitation films (though they began to disappear by the mid-1970s). However, films that dealt with the non-exploitational aspects of black life, such as *Claudine* (1974), *Conrack* (1974) and *The Bingo Long Traveling All-Stars* (1976), did not do well at the box office. With rare exceptions, black films needed a star personality such as Diana Ross (*Lady Sings the Blues*, 1972) or Richard Pryor (*Greased Lightning*, 1977), to get the cross-over audience – whites who would not normally go to see a film about blacks. And although these stars could generally sell a film, they tended to be well-crafted escapist works rather than films that dealt with the psychological and social reality of black life. Hollywood seemed to sense that in the seventies white guilt towards blacks had

begun to disappear and black political and civil rights organisations had lost their potency and power. They now felt it
necessary only to place blacks in minor character roles rather
than to deal with their complex reality. It was a decision which
was in tune with the dictates of the market and the political and
social climate of the 1970s.

It is also important to note that not all the films engaging in a
critique of American society and culture came from the
perspective of minority groups or left-liberal politics. Many
people were appalled in the sixties and early seventies by what
they perceived to be a period of permissiveness and social
breakdown. Their answer was a return to traditional values of
home, family, and law and order. Part of this yearning was
turned by Hollywood into a nostalgia for a lone man with a gun
bringing law and order to an untamed frontier, only this time
that frontier included the city as well. *Death Wish* (1974) and
Walking Tall (1974) were two prime examples of this film genre,
but the best and most archetypal one was Don Siegel's
brilliantly edited *Dirty Harry* (1971), starring Clint Eastwood.

Dirty Harry was a film about an avenging angel or knight of a
San Francisco police inspector, Harry Callahan, whose major
targets besides criminals are the permissiveness of our society
and its laws, and the liberals and politicians who helped create
that social climate. In the film Harry pursues a psychopathic,
hippie killer who has tortured, killed, and even kidnapped a bus
filled with children. Harry is a solitary, lean, indomitable figure
who will not rest or be deterred by mere legalities (like civil
liberties) or rules until he has killed this personification of pure
evil – there are no psychological or social explanations for the
killer's behaviour. Using low-angle and full shots of the
demi-god Harry the film identifies totally with him, making his
superiors seem lame and weak, and Harry's vigilante justice
the only protection against a violent, demonic world. At the end
of the film, in a scene reminiscent of *High Noon*, Harry throws
his badge into the water where the killer's corpse is floating.
Obviously, it is only a *beau geste* for in sequels like *Magnum Force*
(1973) and *The Enforcer* (1976), Harry wages all-out war against
radicals, homosexuals and other flotsam of a permissive
society.[25]

The films of the early seventies provide a good illustration of how long it takes for major cultural changes to register with some degree of subtlety in Hollywood films. Whether or not their critiques were inspired by the right or the left these films were a spill-over from the ideological conflicts and social tensions of the sixties. In a similar fashion the films of the second half of the seventies were a belated acknowledgement of some of the major trends of the early seventies, most particularly the need to bind up the nation's wounds implied in slogans like Nixon's 'bring us together', Ford's 'time of healing' and Carter's 'government as good as its people'.

The film industry, perceiving in turn that its audience genuinely desired some balm for its pain, turned in the main to relentlessly packaging escapist entertainment. Some of the films, such as the Bicentennial blockbuster, *Rocky* (1976), affirmed traditional American values like the Horatio Alger dream of 'rags to riches'. The fairy-tale dimensions of the film were projected both on and off the screen for it was written by an unemployed and practically destitute actor, Sylvester Stallone, who became an overnight sensation and superstar and won an Academy award.

Rocky was a film about a broken-down pug who also moonlights as an enforcer for a mob loan shark. However, Rocky combined the body of a circus strongman with the saintliness of St Francis. He was kind to animals and small children, and gave a break even to those who were behind in their payments to the loan shark. Rocky's big moment comes when the black heavyweight champion grants him a shot at the title. The scenes of his training and his Dionysian struggle with the champion Apollo Creed turn into a powerful evocation and endorsement of the importance of honesty, perseverance and hard work.

Rocky not only revived the Alger myth, it made ethnic, working-class Americans the prime actors and agents of the dream. In Rocky the film had created a character who existed as some pre-psychoanalytic being, a man who could invoke nostalgia for a purer, simpler past. It was possible that, for the general film-going audience, working-class lives had now become a preserve of spontaneity, warmth and masculinity.

In fact the success of *Rocky* made the white working class

fashionable in Hollywood again. The trend took off into solid, commercial hits like *Saturday Night Fever* (1978), a critical success like *Norma Rae* (1979), and less successful films such as *Blue Collar* (1977), *F.I.S.T.* (1978) and *Bloodbrothers* (1978), all of which highlighted working-class characters and situations, though in the main they are more interested in genre conventions than in class realities.[26]

In *Saturday Night Fever* the hero, Tony Manero (John Travolta), conveys on the surface much of the same mixture of macho charisma, gentleness and vulnerability as Rocky. But instead of the heroics taking place in the ring, his arena is the dance floor, where he is the local king of the disco. However, his undulating energy and dynamism on the dance floor do not provide him with a way out of his neighbourhood wasteland. Tony's world consists of a mother and an unemployed construction worker father, both of whom constantly put him down and shout at each other; a pill-popping, gang-banging and fighting, oafish group of friends; and a job without a future as a clerk in a hardware store.

Saturday Night Fever is a more complex and suggestive film than *Rocky*. Though *Rocky* cannot escape touching on certain social realities such as decaying ethnic neighbourhoods and racial conflict (that is, Rocky as 'the great white hope'), it still blurs, even obliterates those tensions in a magical act of transcendence. However, *Saturday Night Fever* allowed much more of the anxieties of working-class life to intrude before submerging them in the romantic music of the Bee Gees and disco scenes shot through multi-coloured filters by a fluidly zooming and panning camera.

In *Saturday Night Fever* Tony, though more sensitive, decent and perceptive than his friends, is not quite another saintly Rocky. His character is built on a blend of crude street humour, macho posturing and self-absorption. He can use and dismiss friends (male and female) without much consciousness of their feelings or existence. The film also touches on working-class sexism, frustration and rage and how socially inadequate working-class people feel, when dealing with upper-middle-class culture. However, the film is still primarily a commercial, escapist work which prefers to keep its eyes averted from the full meaning of these problems and emotions.

In fact, like *Rocky* (though in much more muted fashion) the film offers a second chance to Travolta, a romance with an upwardly mobile secretary, Stephanie (Karen Lee Gorney), and the repudiation of his Brooklyn world for a supposedly more humane and golden existence in Manhattan.[27]

Along with *Rocky*'s affirmation of the American Dream came a revival of the traditional Hollywood theme of the uncommon common man. For example, in Steven Spielberg's *Jaws* (1976), the family man as hero is affirmed amidst blockbuster technical effects and the brilliant building of tension and suspense. Most memorable about *Jaws* are the skilfully edited scenes of a killer shark's attack on a summer resort. However, among the thinly sketched characters is a middle-class, family man, police chief, Martin Brody (Roy Scheider), who battles against the cover ups of the town's corrupt mayor and ultimately kills the shark after the upper-class technologisms of icthyologist Matt Hooper (Richard Dreyfuss) and the working-class machismo of the Ahab-like Quint (Robert Shaw) have failed. *Jaws* implicitly celebrated the virtues of fidelity and family instead of glorifying the heroic loner.[28]

But even *Jaws* was touched with the anxieties of the real world. In George Lucas' *Star Wars* (1977), the ultimate in escapism was achieved by creating a magical setting somewhat similar to the West where heroic action could take place. The audience no longer had to be bothered by images of real streets, problems and people, it could lose itself in outer space. In *Star Wars*, Lucas threw everything he knew into the picture – a catalogue of genre entertainments of the last thirty years – and revitalised America's passion for technology. The film is complete with almost human, cuddly robots, computers and alien beings (looking like an ape version of the *Wizard of Oz*'s Cowardly Lion), and scenes of glorified combat with rocket fighters right out of the Second World War films: all placed in a fantasy galaxy. Lucas' inventiveness is framed within a story of a 'quest' for the 'force' in a hierarchical world which does not only consist of robots, but contains knights, villains in black, princesses and priests, all of which were staples of adventure fiction, comic books and fairy tales. Even if Americans were no longer so willing to follow the lone cowboy as he eternally cleaned up the frontier, they flocked in record numbers to Luke

Skywalker and his cohorts as they blasted through space and shot it out with Darth Vader.[29]

Shoring up this return to past values and genres were films evoking occult dread and divine power. Starting with *The Exorcist* (1973), turned into a terrifying film by William Friedkin (*The French Connection*, 1971), these works began to denounce the sins of modernism and implied that only true faith could ensure peace and tranquillity. *The Exorcist* was viewed by the Jesuit-trained, former USIA writer William Peter Blatty (its scriptwriter) as part of his 'apostolic work'.[30] The film showed how two gentle priests cured the young daughter of a free-thinking, divorced woman of demonic possession after all else, including psychiatry, had failed. Besides preaching the true faith *The Exorcist* and other similar works (for example, *The Omen* (1976), *Exorcist II*) also undermined any sense of individual or moral responsibility. *The Exorcist*, though primarily a work of well-crafted entertainment, still projected in a cold and anti-human tone a belief that the acts of human beings are determined by demonic forces.

Though little intellectual credibility could be given to a belief in demonic forces, *The Exorcist* was symptomatic of a number of Hollywood films of the second half of the decade. In contrast to films of the first half of the decade, which either attacked American capitalism and culture for its corruption, murderousness and creation of ersatz values, or saw criminality aided by liberalism overwhelming traditional institutions, many of the second-half films affirmed traditional American values such as mobility, family, technology and religious belief.

Perhaps the ultimate test of these values was to be seen in how Hollywood handled the Vietnam war. All through the war Hollywood had shied away from any films that dealt directly with the conflict. Despite some films (*Bonnie and Clyde*, *The Wild Bunch*) acting as oblique metaphors for the war, there was doubt whether Hollywood would ever directly confront the issue at all. It was a common assumption, in an industry where appeal to the lowest common denominator is the key to making a profit, that a war that was so divisive and controversial was a recipe for financial disaster.

However, as a number of successful novels and memoirs on the war came out, and people's passions about Vietnam cooled, films dealing with the war seemed less risky. Moreover, in books such as Tim O'Brien's National Book Award-winning novel, *Going After Cacciato* and in Michael Herr's brilliant *Dispatches*, there is a feeling that only a film could convey the nightmarish and absurdist imagery of the war, and make the ultimate statement about Vietnam, integrating it into the national consciousness. Consequently, after the release of a number of smaller films about Vietnam (*Boys in Company C*, 1978, *Tracks*, 1978 and *Go Tell the Spartans*, 1978), the war and its impact were treated in three big-budget films, *Coming Home* (1978), *The Deerhunter* (1978) and *Apocalypse Now* (1979).[31]

Coming Home, directed by Hal Ashby and starring Jane Fonda, Bruce Dern and Jon Voight, was a film about returning veterans in the tradition of *Best Years of Our Lives* and *The Men*. What made this film different was that it did not depict the veterans as men who, though mutilated by the war, were still committed to the goals they supposedly were fighting for. In *Coming Home* the wounds are both physical and psychological, symbolic of the film's pacifistic, anti-war position. In addition, the film's prime focus, the romantic affair between a Marine Corps Captain's wife, Sally Hyde (Jane Fonda), and a paraplegic Vietnam veteran, Luke Martin (Jon Voight), is permeated with the psychological and ideological transformations that people underwent during the war. Furthermore, the suicidal despair of the eager, ambitious Marine Captain Bob Hyde (Bruce Dern), a man without reservations about going off to Vietnam, evoked the alienation and moral disintegration that often accompanied front-line service in Vietnam.

Nevertheless, *Coming Home* remained a safe, humanistic film, more interested in attacking the horrors of war than in the specific moral and political terrors of Vietnam. It contains moving scenes of disabled veterans talking unself-consciously about the war, but it never went to the heart of the nightmare that Hyde's despair suggested. This clearly was not the case with Michael Cimino's *The Deerhunter*. Cimino's controversial epic was alternately condemned ('racist', 'a total lie') or praised ('brilliant', 'emotionally devastating') by critics and Vietnam war correspondents. The film even brought on hostile demonstrations when it won the Academy award in 1978.

The three central figures in *The Deerhunter* are three young steelworkers, Michael (Robert DeNiro), Nicky (Christopher Walken), and Steven (John Savage), from a milltown in Western Pennsylvania who go off without hesitation or questions to fight in Vietnam. These are men who are linked to each other and their ethnic community not by words or ideology, but by a number of visible and invisible strands of ritual and memory. Cimino is in love with ritual and turns every experience (for example, rock songs, drinking and hunting) into an elaborate ceremony. He is more interested in exaltation than in analysis, more concerned with evolving images of a warm, working-class community than with illuminating the social structure and culture of that world. The apotheosis of Cimino's homage to traditional working-class life – an ethos that may have existed only in myth and nostalgia – is the ethnic wedding sequence. It is a lovingly detailed but overextended scene, where the film's major characters sing, dance, brawl and express a sense of camaraderie.

The first half of the film creates a mythic working-class milieu – a more intact and joyous community than ever graced *Rocky* or *Saturday Night Fever*. For even *The Deerhunter*'s steel mill is no 'dark satanic mill' filled with alienated and resentful workers but an elegant monolith where sooty workers labour with gusto and even pleasure. But it is in the second half of the film that Cimino makes his Vietnam statement and has his trio of politically unconscious workers go off to war to face its brutality, pain and horror, and have their connection to each other and their community almost totally torn apart.

The only one of the trio to come out of Vietnam psychologically unscathed is Michael, the deerhunter of the title. Cimino conceives Michael as a working-class aristocrat (like Tony Manero and Rocky), but in the tradition of James Fenimore Cooper's *The Deerslayer*, a man who stands somewhat outside the society and struggles with nature to define his manhood. Michael is pictured as silent, stoical and sexually chaste, a daredevil leader and possessed of a steely will. It is his will that saves the trio when they are tortured in emotionally and politically manipulative but stunningly conceived Russian roulette sessions murderously presided over by their North Vietnamese captors. It is also Michael's will that acts to unite the trio after the nightmare of the war – a mission which is only partially realised.

If the film lacks a conscious coherent political ideology, its total identification and exaltation of Michael's will and heroism has the effect of inverting history, making the Americans guiltless victims and the Vietnamese the aggressors in the war. For although the film evokes the conflict with graphic and violent immediacy and constructs metaphors (for example, Nicky as a suicidal Russian roulette specialist) which have a great deal of emotional resonance, the Vietnamese are seen as 'the other', without exception as either demonic or decadent variations of 'the yellow peril'. The film seems to suffer from a case of political and moral amnesia, forgetting all about America's war crimes and imperial guilt for the war. For it was the Americans who were the aggressors and extended the conflict, who carpet-bombed and napalmed the Vietnamese and adulterated and destroyed the social fabric of South Vietnam.

In addition, the final scene where Michael and his friends gather after Nicky's funeral to sing 'God Bless America', affirming a supposedly tattered but intact American will and community, self-consciously tries to nullify all the destruction and despair that have come before. In the *Deerhunter* this ritual of reconciliation is just as severed as the war from its historical and social roots; the film is more interested in metaphors than in confronting the political reality of the war.[32]

Despite its intellectual limitations and distortions, *The Deerhunter* did give some sense of the spiritual desolation and destruction that Vietnam caused for Americans. However, the film not only raised a great deal of controversy, but was often taken by audiences as a homage to the American troops and cause. As a result it made the final release of Francis Ford Coppola's *Apocalypse Now* (1979) that much more eagerly awaited. It seemed that this film would be that final statement about the war that so many people wanted to see. Coppola reinforced these expectations when he equated the making of the film with the war itself. He said, 'we made it (*Apocalypse Now*) the way America made war in Vietnam. There were too many of us, too much money and equipment, and little by little we went insane'.

Apocalypse Now was loosely based on Joseph Conrad's *Heart of Darkness*, particularly its evocation of the emotional and moral rot of imperialism. In *Apocalypse Now* Coppola deletes the first part of the novella and emphasises the portion describing the journey up river, and the final confrontation between Marlow (Willard in the film) and Kurtz. Willard (Martin Sheen) is a burnt-out government hit man with six kills to his credit, whose mission is to terminate with extreme prejudice the command of Colonel Kurtz (Marlon Brando), changed from an ivory hunter who 'had kicked himself loose of the earth' into a rogue Green Beret Colonel who had set himself up as a God waging a brutal private war in the Cambodian jungle.

Using Willard's pilgrimage as a framework Coppola presented a spaced-out, surreal Vietnam – the war as an absurdist epic. The film is filled with spectacular scenes touched with a sense of the absurd and mad: an exhilarating *Gotterdammerung* helicopter attack led by Colonel Kilgore (Robert Duvall as an exaggerated version of General Patton), to whom napalm is the perfume of victory and the purpose of destroying a Vietcong village is to discover the perfect wave for surfing; the revolt of sex-starved soldiers after being tantalised and provoked by a garish USO bump and grind show of Playboy bunnies; and an officerless and forgotten platoon of black GIs despairingly shooting into the darkness in the 'asshole of the world'. These set pieces and a number of Coppola's other horrible but beautiful images grant the film great visual power and a genuine feeling for the chaos and incoherence of the war.

Unfortunately, the ultimate confrontation between Kurtz and an empty and exhausted Willard is anti-climactic. There is too much straining for significance, too many gnomic and pretentious utterances from Kurtz, whose literary allusions range from Eliot's *The Hollow Men* to the *Golden Bough*. There is no interaction or connection between Willard and Kurtz, just Coppola trying to sum up the powerful, imaginative and farcical images from the first two-thirds of the film into one supposedly profound symbol and idea, attempting to transform the physical into the metaphysical.

Kurtz is portrayed by Coppola in almost Nietzschean terms as a man who trades in gnostic tales of NLF soldiers hacking off the arms of villagers inoculated by Americans, demonstrating a 'will which is crystalline in its purity' and indulging in aphoristic comments like 'judgement defeats us, we must make friends with moral terror'. In constructing the character of Kurtz, Coppola does touch on the American 'will to power' in Vietnam, but ultimately his philosophic musings turn him into such a moral (metaphysical) abstraction that we lose sight of Vietnam and the way the American will ran amuck there (for example, the Kilgore scene), and instead get a vaporous notion of civilisation's madness. Indeed *Apocalypse Now* universalises the conflict by making its terror a part of the human condition rather than a result of a particular historical and social reality.

In addition, Coppola had a great deal of difficulty concluding the film (he experimented with alternate endings), for his startling and original images could only carry him so far. The unwillingness of Willard to assume Kurtz's role as deity and the death of Kurtz and the bombing of his temple can either consciously or unconsciously be seen as suggesting that America has decided to abdicate its imperial pretensions. It is as if in the destruction of Kurtz America's sense of invulnerability has been exorcised without its ever confronting the specific guilt and responsibility that the government had for Vietnam.

There is a German proverb that states that a war creates three armies: an army of cripples, an army of beggars and an army of the unemployed. The Vietnam war had created a fourth army: one of film-makers. But these are directors who have substituted a gift for inventive metaphors and ingenious images for the ability to pierce the political heart of darkness.[32]

Of course, Hollywood has rarely tried to penetrate that heart, usually constructing well-honed conventions and ceremonies to neutralise and mute those anxieties and truths. The Academy award ceremonies of 1978 was an occasion where Hollywood utilised its genius for shaping public rituals and neutralising what was politically or emotionally difficult. There John Wayne (in his last public appearance before his death) was called to present the Oscar for best film to Michael Cimino for *The Deerhunter*. In the sixties and seventies Wayne had become synonymous with the traditional American verities, and with a virulent, jingoistic right-wing politics. Though *The Deerhunter* was clearly no left-wing film, its alienated, maimed and tortured soldiers (though there was still a stoical hero) enveloped in a futile war, were a far cry from the tough, confident, uncomplicated fighting men portrayed by Wayne in *They were Expendable* (1949) and *The Sands of Iwo Jima*. The ceremony brought together the two Hollywoods: Wayne who had gone through the ranks from bit player to icon and Cimino, who without the long apprenticeship common to the old studio system (he had made only one previous film, *Thunderbolt and Lightfoot*, 1974) found himself with a multi-million-dollar picture in his hands. As it had done so often in the past, Hollywood had found the appropriate ceremony to absorb, exploit and neutralise what could possibly be seen as deviant and new.

Even without the death of John Wayne giving the decade a symbolic capstone, the seventies were an end to an era in American films. Gone forever were even the remnants of the old studio production system, and in its place the studio had become a financial clearing house, dependent on independent producers rather than a rationalised, studio-run assembly line. The old Hollywood which could produce family pictures cheerily affirming mobility, success, family and patriotism had also passed. Its values now stood open to question, and its films were touched with a greater sense of uncertainty and bewilderment than in the past. However, none of these changes meant that the Hollywood conventions had been destroyed. It was still a world where the big-budget films were dominant, where stars called the shots as much as they ever did, and where television provided most of the creative models (such as situation comedies). Nevertheless, in its faltering and confused way, Hollywood still had the magic and potency to create a world which both hinted at and obscured the reality of the American ethos.

6. The Eighties

ALTHOUGH neither of the authors has any special access to crystal balls (or any real talent for predicting the future) there still remain one or two cinematic trends that have already manifested themselves in the early eighties. Of course, whether or not they ripen and become dominant themes of the decade remains an open question.

Underlying these trends is the overriding 1980s phenomenon of Reaganism. It is a phenomenon that might best be summarised by reference to an anecdote (perhaps apocryphal) that involves Reagan's old studio boss, Jack Warner. According to this tale, when Warner was told in 1966 that the Republican Party had nominated Reagan for governor of California his agitated comment was: 'No, No that's wrong, Jimmy Stewart for governor, Reagan for the governor's best friend'.

Obviously, this was as much a comment on Reagan's Hollywood career, where he often played the hero's best friend, than any implied criticism of the astuteness of California's GOP. Nonetheless it also serves as an apt comment on Reagan's political philosophy, which has made him the best friend in government that the American military-corporate power structure ever had. Indeed the 25 per cent tax cut enacted in his first year in office delighted business, as the almost 10 per cent increase over inflation in military spending pleased the Pentagon. Similarly his cuts in domestic spending – health care, low-cost housing and income maintenance programmes – elated conservatives, who saw them as the beginning of their long-hoped-for counter-offensive against five decades of the Welfare State.

Unfortunately, the Reagan economic policy, quickly redubbed 'Reaganomics' (critics named it 'voodoo economics') in exchange for its original 'supply side' title, resulted in the worst bout of unemployment (helping to create a subculture of homeless people who wandered the streets of American cities), bankruptcies and corporate deficits since the 'Great Depression'. Nevertheless, despite the growing income gap between the rich and poor and the failure of what were essentially his 'trickle down' economic tenets, Reagan rigidly held on to his beliefs, shoring them up with anecdotes about welfare 'cheats' and a philosophy of voluntarism that seemed to owe as much to Frank Capra (a Capra without a social conscience) as to Herbert Hoover.

Nor was this film-based political vision confined to economic affairs. In foreign policy, in what was called his 'Darth Vader' speech, Reagan referred to the Soviet Union as an 'evil empire', and extended the *Star Wars* metaphor even further by justifying his military build-up with allusions to as-yet unbuilt space weapons that would presumably deter aggression. It seemed finally as if America had got a president who not only embedded, but was deeply committed to, all the crack-brained fantasies and empty rhetoric peddled by Hollywood ever since it became the centre of America's popular culture.

Obviously, Reagan's sabre rattling had a disquieting effect on America and its allies. If nothing else it helped relaunch anti-nuclear and disarmament campaigns that had lain dormant for a number of years. In small towns and large cities people all over the world began again to protest against the Strangelovian nuclear policies of the last forty-five years. In a similar fashion, by unleashing so called free-market forces, particularly on the air, land and workplaces of America (dismantling the Environmental Protection Administration (EPA) by placing people in charge who served the special interests), Reagan incurred the ire of the nation's environmentalists.

Nonetheless, despite these problems, mid-term election losses, and an unemployment rate of over 10 per cent, Reagan continued to gain the approval of the majority of Americans. Much of it had to do with his undoubted charm, his quickness with a quip and his calming nice-guy demeanour, media assets which, when coupled with his actor's talent as a 'Great Communicator' (he reads shamelessly from cue cards), marked him out as a favourite to regain the Presidency in 1984. It clearly said something about the American public's obsession with imagery and personality (the Hollywood effect) that this politically unreflective and callow figure could continue to remain popular in America.[1]

However, it was not clear that his old industry reaped any benefits from his policies. Not that times were bad. In fact, overall income and profits were up for most of the major studios. Yet, as always in an insecure industry, anxieties were heightened by Reagan's economic policies, especially since they swelled interest rates. Since the life blood of Hollywood is borrowed capital, the number of films produced each year suffered a severe cut back. At the same time, Hollywood looked for economic shelter, usually in the arms of huge conglomerates that had enough internal excess capital to avoid high interest rates. Thus the conglomeratisation of Hollywood that started in the sixties and seventies continued apace, with the gobbling up of previously unattached studios like Columbia (Coca Cola) and the mergers of old giants like MGM and United Artists. In addition, these conglomerates were positioning themselves in the film business to take advantage of what they believed was the coming explosion of new telecommunications technology (cable, cassettes, video discs), which they hoped would grant them the same opportunities for profit that allowed Warner Communications to garner more profits in 1982 from its Atari video games than from its film division.

Meanwhile, industry insecurity was also heightened by the failure of Michael Cimino's intellectually empty and inchoate western epic, *Heaven's Gate* (1980), a total economic and critical disaster. Suddenly studios were calling into question the whole policy of allowing big-budget laissez faire to directors with only one or two hits to their credit. A search was initiated for highly marketable properties based on pre-sold reputations – sequels like *Superman II* and *Rocky III* (a film which exploits racial fears and stereotypes by creating a villain who is a brutal, black boxer with an ominous, baleful look).[2]

It was perhaps this insecurity and the quest for bankable commodities that made it easier for Robert Redford to direct a film. Redford had been the producer of well-received and even financially successful films like *Downhill Racer* (1960), *The Candidate* (1972), and *All the President's Men* (1976), and this time decided himself to direct a film based on Judith Guest's novel, *Ordinary People* (1980).

To some extent the material of *Ordinary People* was made to order for Redford with his Hollywood image of the WASP golden boy in films like *The Way We Were* (1973) and *The Candidate* (1972). The film conveyed the dark side of the upper-middle-class, suburban WASP world. One in which the placid, comfortable life of the Jarret family of suburban Chicago is disrupted by the accidental death of their eldest son Buck, and the subsequent suicide attempt and hospitalisation in a mental hospital of his guilt-ridden, bright and sensitive younger brother, Conrad (Timothy Hutton).

The villain of the film is not the middle-class materialism or the conformist wasteland of the suburbs of a film like *The Graduate*, but WASP repression and control as epitomised by Conrad's handsome, compulsively neat mother, Beth (Mary Tyler Moore). She is a woman so obsessed with appearances and so fearful of allowing her emotions to get out of control that she deals with the family tragedy by remarking that: 'We'd have been alright if there hadn't been any mess'. The Jarret family 'mess', and, in particular, the terror in Conrad's eyes, only begins to be worked out when Dr Berger (Judd Hirsch), Conrad's warm, commonsensical, and iconoclastic Jewish psychiatrist, starts getting through to him. Berger not only helps the self-lacerating Conrad to get in touch with his feelings about himself and his mother, but as a bonus shakes his passive, somewhat unconscious, but loving father Calvin (Donald Sutherland) out of his bondage to his wife's rigidity.

Ordinary People is a small, intelligent film which elicits excellent performances from its actors, and has an assured feel for the cocktail chatter and the green lawns and back yards of the insulated, white Lake Forest suburb where the film was made. However, the film is primarily a work of two shots and interiors, a domestic work much less interested in the world of the upper middle class (there is no evidence that Calvin's values are much different from Beth's) than in the tensions of family life. Despite subtle touches such as Dr Berger's office becoming darker as Conrad gains more insight into his problems, the film is marred by Redford's habit of sometimes reducing the complexities of familial conflict to pat formulae.

From Conrad getting just the right, jargon-free (for example, 'Something bugging you') psychiatrist, to his meeting up with the most understanding and loveliest of high-school co-ed girlfriends (Elizabeth McGovern), the film has a tendency to be facile. However, what helps *Ordinary People* transcend some of its clichés and melodramatic contrivances (the boating accident itself) is Redford's gift for having his actors use their faces and body movements to convey a wide range of emotions. In what was an especially inspired bit of casting, Redford got Mary Tyler Moore (America's sitcom sweetheart) to play against type, and she gave a performance which avoids turning her frigid, golf-playing, napkin-folding mother into a mere stereotype. She is able to communicate successfully the profound desperation and insecurity that lies underneath her need to cleave to the surfaces of life and to coerce the people around her to do the same.[3]

However, though her ability to project feelings of anxiety adds nuance and dimension to the role, the mother is still the villain of the film. It is she who is unwilling to contemplate changing and going to therapy, and even at the end of the film she is incapable of giving any affection or love to Conrad. Therefore she must bear primary responsibility for Conrad's problems and must leave the home – allowing the family to be reborn as a male preserve. It is her cold-bloodedness and egoism that links *Ordinary People* with sophisticated, often unconscious feminist backlash elements inherent in films like *Kramer vs. Kramer* and even in some ways *Tootsie* (1982). Like the wife in *Kramer*, Beth flees familial responsibility and leaves the husband to assume the nurturing, maternal role. Indeed in both films we are left with the image of women (though they are very different people) either as irresponsible and uncaring, or, especially in Beth's case, as devourers.

Tootsie, of course, is a very different sort of work from the other films we have linked it with. It was one of the big box office hits of 1982, a genuinely clever and funny film with beautifully timed gags, witty one liners, and a virtuoso performance by Dustin Hoffman. It is built around the classic comic gambit of the man who dresses up as a woman, and then cannot have his identity revealed (for example, *Some Like it Hot*, 1959). However, Hoffman and the film's director, Sydney

Pollock, were not satisfied with merely making a film which left audiences howling, and they began to make serious claims for the film as an exploration of gender and sexual roles.

Tootsie is the sort of film that can baldly state that each of us carries both maleness and femaleness, and that a man can acquire greater sensitivity and humanness by getting in touch with his femaleness. It also touches on other feminist issues and insights by dramatising the insults and patronising behaviour constantly bestowed upon women at work by their bosses and, of course, asserts that women must stand up for their dignity. However, despite the film's self-conscious feminism the reality of *Tootsie* is much more conventional than its ambitions. As Dorothy Michaels, soap-opera star, Hoffman continuously affirms his maleness beneath the female impersonation; there is little sense of Hoffman having truly experienced his female side. And Dorothy Michael's feminism is troubling since it ends up that the strongest and, in fact, the only feminist in the film is a man, the other female characters being either neurotically insecure or vulnerable and dependent on a man to provide direction. *Tootsie* is a skilful, entertaining film which breaks little new ground, for it ultimately demonstrates how a man can become a feminist and leave the traditional sexual patterns in place. Just as in *Kramer vs. Kramer* and *Ordinary People*, the new hero-heroine of *Tootsie*'s brand of feminism turns out to be a man.[4]

Though small personal works like *Ordinary People* and a farce with pretensions to social significance like *Tootsie* were popular in the early eighties, probably more symptomatic of the period were the works of Steven Spielberg. In the seventies Spielberg directed blockbuster hits like *Jaws* and his *Close Encounters of the Third Kind* (1977) almost singlehandedly resurrected the fortunes of Columbia Pictures. But after the failure of his comedy *1941* (1980), his career seemed on the wane, until aided by his friend and USC schoolmate, George Lucas (the film's Executive Producer), he directed *Raiders of the Lost Ark* (1981).

As in his previous films – the hunt for the malevolent shark in *Jaws*, the extra-terrestrials in *Close Encounters*, and the Japanese submarine in *1941* – *Raiders* is basically a story about a quest. In this case it deals with the competition between an intrepid and invulnerable American archaeologist, Indiana Jones (Harrison

Ford), and the Nazis to find the lost ark of the covenant, which will give its possessor unlimited power.

Although the film does go in for an awesome, though nonsensical, religious display at its finale, and there is talk of the gleaming gold ark having infinite power beyond man's understanding, its appeal and even its subtext, lie not with these elements, but with its reflection of the old Hollywood and its skilled manipulation of an audience's need to feel anxiety, lose itself in harmless fantasy, and become nostalgic.

In fact, from the film's opening credit, where the Paramount fades into a snow-covered Andean peak, to a fadeout, when it recreates the final scene in *Citizen Kane*, we are treated to a whole host of images and themes garnered from old Hollywood – particularly the cliffhanging serials of the thirties. Apropos of this genre, the whip-snapping, unreflective Indiana and his hard-drinking, tough but dependent girlfriend, Marion (Karen Allen), face down poison darts, snakes, rotting corpses, assorted gun-toting villains, and finally out-smart and out-fight the inhuman Nazi hordes. The upshot of it all is not so much to reassure us about good triumphing over evil – Indiana's only real commitment is to adventure and acquiring the ark (even Marion is an afterthought) – but to enclose us in a claustrophobic world of action for its own sake, thus rendering *Raiders* to as close as a film can come to being a children's comic book.[5]

It is that very same child that exists in all of us that Spielberg appealed to so imaginatively and skilfully in *E.T.* (1982). Written by Melissa Mathison, who wrote the scenario for the lyrical children's film *Black Stallion*, *E.T.* managed to hit on a mine of primal fantasy. It is basically the story of a benign extra-terrestrial (who looks very much like one of the aliens in *Close Encounters*) who is left behind when his space ship takes off without him, and a young boy, Elliot (Henry Thomas), who befriends, protects and helps him return to his home. The story is as simple and familiar as any about a boy and his pet dog. However, there is more to the film than a bare sketch of the plot would suggest. *E.T.* contains numerous references and images invoking children's films (like *Bambi*, 1943; *Mary Poppins*, 1964; *Peter Pan*, 1953; *Meet Me in St. Louis*, 1944). In addition, the film carries a feeling of religiosity that alternately transforms the cute, doll-like extra-terrestrial into a loving father substitute and, possibly pushing it a bit too far, a Christ figure (E.T. dies and is resurrected in the midst of a family where the mother's name happens to be Mary).

Of course the qualities that made *E.T.* a great commercial success (within less than a year of its release it was assured of becoming one of the top grossing films of all time) went far beyond its *Bambi*-like forest imagery or its religious resonances. Among the most significant of these was the emphasis it gave to the need all of us have for unwavering affection – here conveyed in the spiritual union between E.T. and Elliot. Pervading the whole film was Spielberg's commitment to child-like innocence, reinforced by his ability to visualise the world the way a child does.

As a result of the film's emphasis on a child's perspective adults and adult authority are either treated warily or distrusted altogether. Even Keys (Peter Coyote), the benevolent and sympathetic head of the government scientists sent out to find E.T., wants to subject him to scientific scrutiny, and that alone places him in the adult realm. None of the adult males in the film (they are the real aliens), including Keys, are ever shown beyond their midriffs, they are a faceless, ominous, almost malevolent group. Elliot's mother is depicted as ineffectual (she has difficulty coping with being a single parent), and his father as irresponsible (causing Elliot distress by running off to Mexico with another woman). In *E.T.* the children ultimately triumph over the adults with E.T. eluding their grasp and reaching his home, the victory of feeling over rational and scientific thought.

Though *E.T.* was essentially a fairy tale (sometimes a bit too cute and sentimental for its own good) – a film whose meaning is much less significant than the feelings it elicits – its general mood paralleled a number of cultural tendencies in early eighties' America. In its affirmation of innocence, its simple optimism, and its distrust of authority (particularly the state) it unconsciously mirrored some of the certainties and pieties offered to the American public by Ronald Reagan. Indeed both E.T. and Ronald Reagan were eminently lovable, and just as Spielberg's Elliot found solace from his problems in a fantastic creature Reagan mouthed platitudes about traditional values, and fled the complexities inherent in bringing about social change or reshaping the economy.[6]

The fact that the audience also shared this nostalgia for old verities need not rest solely on the election returns, but can be confirmed from the grosses and awards to a film like *On Golden Pond* (1981). In fact, if nothing else, *On Golden Pond* with its saccharine shots of rippling water and loon-filled lakes evoked the aura of a Norman Rockwell painting. Despite the banal imagery, the film did have an important theme and moments of truth about a rite of passage – ageing and the confrontation with dying. Nevertheless, by casting Henry Fonda and Katherine Hepburn in the leading roles as the 80-year-old, ailing Norman Thayer and his radiant, vital wife Ethel, the film paid less attention to gerontology than to Hollywood iconography.

It is not that Fonda's portrayal of the dying Norman was not a fitting culmination to a brilliant career. In fact his characterisation of the surly curmudgeon (with a soft streak) who utters lines like, 'I think I'll read a new book – see if I can finish it before I'm finished. Maybe a novelette', is letter perfect. Likewise is his confusion and anxiety when a well-known path suddenly becomes unknown to him, due to his failing memory.

It was not the characters or the neatly turned, sentimental narrative that drew audiences. What did was the teaming of Fonda and Hepburn, and the cinematic memories it evoked of her co-starring roles with icons like Grant, Tracy and Wayne, and their combined five decades of starring roles from Mary, Queen of Scots to Tom Joad and Mr Roberts. In addition, in casting herself as his estranged daughter Chelsea, Jane Fonda stirred resonances of her real-life, often embattled relationship with her father. Finally, it also gave Hollywood the chance to make amends to an actor who had given so much to the industry and audience over the years by granting him an Academy award for best actor.

The long overdue award to Fonda (Hepburn also won for best actress) was yet another symptom of Hollywood doting on its past. The problem was that this tendency was more than mere nostalgia, for it indicated not just a sentimental longing for the past, but an active use of its ideas and images in lieu of any new subjects, themes or forms. Thus Hollywood's yearning after its past almost seemed symptomatic of a more general longing for an America of a vigorous work ethic and powerful, growing industries, whose policy of speaking softly and carrying a big stick was enough to keep any foreign government (at least the Latin American ones) in line. It was a simpler, more buoyant and heroic past which stood in sharp contrast to a contemporary America where smokestack industries decayed and closed leaving its workforce standing on unemployment lines, and a seemingly growing number of Central American Fidelistas thumbing their noses at American power.[7]

To some extent it was this yearning after a heroic past that contributed to a decidedly peripheral, but still a minor trend in the early eighties – the impulse to make epic films dealing with grand themes. It was a thread that ran through *Heaven's Gate* (1980), a muddled, inarticulate attempt to deal with class warfare in the American West, and Milos Forman's respectful, intelligent but stolid effort in *Ragtime* (1981), based on E. L. Doctorow's jaunty, ironic, cinematic novel of the same name, to deal with the American success myth and American racism: a trend that finally regained some critical (if not real economic) respectability with Warren Beatty's *Reds* (1981).

In many ways *Reds* was as much a personal film for Warren Beatty as *Ordinary People* was for Robert Redford. Like Redford, Beatty's previous successes as the producer-star of *Bonnie and Clyde* (1967), *Shampoo* (1975), and *Heaven Can Wait* (1978) ensured him the industry clout necessary to make a film about, of all things, an American radical and communist. Also in line with Redford, Beatty's film (albeit to a lesser extent) was inspired by personal experience. In the late sixties Beatty had taken a trip to Russia where, whenever he met older communists, they told him how much he physically resembled John Reed. When he returned home, Beatty dived into researching Reed, which set off an almost two-decades-long campaign to do a film about him.[8]

Ultimately, it was a combination of this personal obsession coupled with his awareness of what made for success and failure in the film business that deeply influenced *Reds*. First of all, Beatty (who won an Oscar for direction) decided to limit the focus of the film to the last four years of Reed's life: concentrating on his love affair and marriage to Louise Bryant

(Diane Keaton): their experience and reporting of the Russian Revolution; and Reed's subsequent commitment to building an American Communist Party. Of course this left out important aspects of Reed's life: his equally intense involvement with wealthy Mabel Dodge Luhan (who ran a salon in the Village); and his participation in the Mexican Revolution and the IWW struggles (both only briefly glimpsed). In addition, the portrayal of Louise as a poor little woman who clings to her man offended many feminists who saw her as much more forceful, defined and talented than the Keaton role conveyed.

Significant as these omissions were, even more glaring was how basically safe the film truly was – especially formally. Of course Beatty faced an insurmountable problem in making a commercially viable film with a 35 million dollar budget which at the same time treated two American communists sympathetically. In making *Reds*, except for his inspired use of the 'witnesses', Beatty never strayed beyond the conventional romantic epic. In fact, despite its references to Stieglitz photos and Eisenstein's *Ten Days that Shook the World*, it owed its greatest debt to David Lean. In one episode Beatty had Louise, in her attempt to unite with an imprisoned Reed, doing a pointless reprise of Dr Zhivago's trek across the frozen tundra to Lara. Also the film had a tendency to transform the chaos of the Revolution and the squalor and poverty of War Communism into Hollywood operatics and glamour. In *Reds* historical credibility is sacrificed so that the Revolution can become a carefully choreographed magical tableau.[9]

Unfortunately, in this quest for commercially viable elements Beatty often skirted perilously close to romantic comedy, complete with cute puppy dogs, and running gags like Reed bumping into a chandelier. However, the most problematic element in the film was the characterisation of and especially the relationship between Reed and Bryant. It is difficult to say if the problem lay in the acting of Beatty and Keaton, the script, the direction, or a combination of all three. Keaton and Beatty work hard, and Keaton does try to drop her Annie Hall mannerisms. She is even able to infuse some complexity into the role when she communicates both her insecurity and her resentment at being treated as a mere adjunct to Reed during their early Village days (especially when Emma Goldman curtly dismisses her as she fumbles for words). There is also nothing in her performance of the passion and sensuality of the woman whose touch, according to Eugene O'Neill, could set you afire. (Indeed the only time she conveys a bit of that fire is in her scenes with O'Neill, played with great brio and force by Jack Nicholson.) In addition, the scene where Bryant begins to offer trenchant political criticism of the relationship between the American Communist Party and the working class feels so incongruous (nothing in the film has prepared one for Bryant projecting this level of political sophistication) that it is almost as if a ventriloquist's dummy is talking.[10]

Beatty in turn struggles to capture a life of the scale that Reed lived – his romantic individualism, his contentiousness, and the passion and intensity of his political commitment. However, though he makes him an attractive figure, nowhere does one get the sense of a man whom Walter Lippmann described as: 'Many men at once . . . there is no line between the play of his fancy and the responsibility to fact: he is for the time the person he imagines himself to be'.[11] In fact Beatty, with his boyish charm, winsome smiles and sheepish looks is not so much protean as eager to please. And the complicated, painful, and contradictory relationship between Reed and Bryant, which is made the focus of much of the film, is superficial and seen primarily from the outside, through meetings, partings and passionate reconciliations, rather than through illuminating its intricate internal life and motivation.

Nevertheless, despite these limitations the film overall is both stirring and provocative. First of all because it was one of the few times a Hollywood film had at its centre an appealing hero who was fully committed to a left politics. And secondly because it provided both a sympathetic handling of the euphoria of the Russian Revolution, and made the history of the American left accessible and engaging. Even though there is too much of a concentration on the relationship between Bryant and Reed, there is still a sense of two people living on the rim of a new world which will usher in a cultural and sexual revolution as well as a political one. Of course it is corny to hear *The Internationale* played with such exaltation while Reed and Bryant make love and the Bolsheviks take over the government. However, it is also moving to see an image of politics evoked (more American sixties than Communist Party) which merges the personal and the political, as much a revolt against bourgeois culture as against capitalism itself.

Coinciding with this image of a utopian – thoroughly romantic, impulsive and exhilarating – political commitment, is the most biting, incisive, and lucid political dialogue to appear in an American film. Undoubtedly the contribution of Beatty's screenwriting collaborator, British leftist playwright Trevor Griffiths (*Comedians*) there are moments (particularly in the film's second half, chronicling Reed's political battles within the American left and with the Comintern) that carry a dialectical electricity. For instance, in one especially insightful moment a weary and disillusioned Emma Goldman (Maureen Stapleton) and Reed debate the effects of the Russian Revolution. Goldman attacks the decline of the revolution into tyranny, stating that: 'The dream we had is dying, Jack. The centralized state has all the power. They're putting anarchists like me in jail, exterminating all dissenters. I want no part of it.' To which, justifying himself, Reed replies: 'What did you think anyway? It was all going to work right away? It's war, Emma. And we have to fight it with discipline, terror, firing squads – or give up.' Then pausing, and expressing his own internal conflicts and misgivings, Reed says something with as much relevance to himself as to her: 'Otherwise what has your life meant?'[12]

Unfortunately, when this sort of exchange is fused with brief portraits of Reed's political struggles with Comintern ideologues and Czars Zinoviev (played by chic Polish-born novelist Jerzy Kosinski) and Radek there was not so much the image of a man analysing and brooding over the nature of the revolutionary process, or of a man conflicted between the Bohemian writer and the disciplined revolutionary in himself, but the simpler, less introspective and less intellectual question: whether or not Reed was ultimately disenchanted with the revolution. It was not that Beatty did not bravely begin to pose the other questions, but the film (being a commercial work) never truly pursued them. Of course, even the question of his disenchantment is never really answered, and is to an extent made to seem somewhat less significant (implicitly rather than explicitly) by the only genuine unconventional formal technique (a chorus and distancing device) in the film – the use of 'witnesses' who were contemporaries of Reed and Bryant.

Like 'petals on a wet black bough',[13] as one critic, quoting Ezra Pound, referred to them, the moving, intelligent, aged faces and voices of Adela Rogers St. John, Rebecca West, Dora Russell, Henry Miller and other famous and once-famous figures comment on Reed and Bryant ('I'd forgotten all about them. Were they Socialists?') and their times ('There was as much fucking then as there is today'). And the one inescapable conclusion drawn from these meandering and fragmented comments is the elusiveness and selectivity of human memory. As a result, whether Reed would have turned against the revolution (as many of his friends like Max Eastman did) is probably less important than the larger truth that a person's historical place and role is difficult to discover and define. Thus, if nothing else *Reds* at least rescued the figures of Reed and Bryant from historical obscurity and assured them a place in popular mythology.

In the final analysis, despite its waning economic significance, it is this very power to create resonant, almost instantaneous cultural myths that Hollywood still retains. It is for this element alone, if for nothing else, that the Hollywood film bears watching as an important barometer of America's dreams and desires and of changes in its cultural and social values. It is also possible that the new technology of video cassettes and cable television which now threatens the industry may force Hollywood to create a more variegated, imaginative and adventurous product. Even though we have argued in this volume that Hollywood film and its mythology have been characterised by a growing sense of despair and alienation over the last four decades (in the eighties even beginning to feed on its own mythology), yet who is so complacent and self-confident that he or she can be certain of the way both our collective future and the future of the little world of film will unfold?

Notes

1. INTRODUCTION

1. A. Sarris, 'Hobgoblins of Reality', *The Village Voice* (21–27 January 1981) p. 45.
2. Ibid.
3. Erwin Panofsky, 'Style and Medium in the Motion Pictures', in G. Mast and M. Cohen (eds), *Film Theory and Criticism* (New York: Oxford University Press, 1974) p. 152.
4. Ibid.
5. John E. O'Connor and Martin A. Jackson (eds), *American History/American Film: Interpreting the Hollywood Image* (New York: Frederick Ungar, 1979) p. x.
6. Siegfried Kracauer, *From Caligari to Hitler: A Psychological History of the German Film*, 3rd ed. (Princeton, New Jersey: Princeton University Press, 1970) p. 6.
7. Stuart Hall and Paddy Whannel, *The Popular Arts* (New York: Pantheon, 1965) p. 28.
8. Raymond Williams, *Communications*, 3rd ed. (London: Pelican, 1976) p. 11.
9. Michael Wood, *America in the Movies; or, 'Santa Maria, It Had Slipped My Mind!'* (New York: Basic Books, 1975) p. 11.
10. James Agee, *Agee on Film; Reviews and Comments* (Boston: Beacon Press, 1966) p. 23.

2. THE FORTIES

1. Godfrey Hodgson, *America in Our Time: From World War II to Nixon, What Happened and Why* (New York: Vintage Books, 1978) pp. 17–64.
2. Ibid., p. 20.
3. Ibid., p. 54.
4. Eric F. Goldman, *The Crucial Decade – and After, America, 1945–1960* (New York: Vintage Books, 1960).
5. Ibid., pp. 46–70.
6. Stephen E. Ambrose, *Rise to Globalism: American Foreign Policy 1938–1970* (Baltimore, Maryland: Penguin Books, 1971) pp. 102–35.
7. Ibid., pp. 136–66.
8. Dean Acheson, *Present at the Creation* (New York: W. W. Norton, 1969) p. 297.
9. Ambrose, *Rise to Globalism*, pp. 136–66.
10. Alistair Cooke, *A Generation on Trial* (Baltimore, Maryland: Penguin Books, 1952).
11. Walter Goodman, *The Committee: The Extraordinary Career of the House Committee on Un-American Activities* (Baltimore, Maryland: Penguin Books, 1969) pp. 207–25.
12. Ibid., p. 300.

13. Cooke, *A Generation on Trial*, pp. 337–41.

14. Charles Higham and Joel Greenberg, *Hollywood in the Forties* (New York: Paperback Library, 1970) p. 18.

15. James Agee, *Agee on Film: Reviews and Comments* (Boston: Beacon Press, 1966) p. 173.

16. Franklin Fearing, 'Warriors Return: Normal or Neurotic', *Hollywood Quarterly* (October, 1945) pp. 91–109.

17. Agee, *Agee on Film*, p. 229.

18. Abe Polonsky, 'The Best Years of Our Lives: A Review', *Hollywood Quarterly* (April, 1947) pp. 91–2.

19. Frank Capra, *The Name Above the Title* (New York: Bantam, 1972) pp. 418–26.

20. Higham and Greenberg, *Hollywood in the Forties*, pp. 19–39.

21. Ibid.

22. Molly Haskell, *From Reverence to Rape: The Treatment of Women in the Movies* (Baltimore, Maryland: Penguin Books, 1974) pp. 153–88.

23. Ibid., pp. 189–230.

24. Ibid.

25. Barbara Deming, *Running Away From Myself: A Dream Portrait of America Drawn From the Films of the Forties* (New York: Grossman Publishers, 1969) p. 6.

26. Joseph G. Goulden, *The Best Years, 1945–1950* (New York: Atheneum, 1976).

27. Donald Bogle, *Toms, Coons, Mulattoes, Mammies and Bucks* (New York: Bantam, 1973).

28. Peter Roffman and Jim Purdy, *The Hollywood Social Problem Film* (Bloomington, Indiana: Indiana University Press, 1981).

29. Hugh Fordin, *The World of Entertainment! Hollywood's Greatest Musicals* (Garden City, New York: Doubleday, 1975).

30. Richard Dyer, 'Entertainment and Utopia', in R. Altman (ed.), *Genre: The Musical* (London: Routledge & Kegan Paul, 1981) pp. 175–89.

3. THE FIFTIES

1. Eric F. Goldman, *The Crucial Decade – And After, America, 1945–1960* (New York: Vintage Books, 1960).

2. Ibid., pp. 202–11.

3. Richard Rovere, *Senator Joseph McCarthy*, rev. ed. (New York: Harper and Row, 1973).

4. Ibid.

5. Ronald Steel, 'Two Cheers for Ike', *The New York Review of Books* (24 September 1981) pp. 10–12.

6. Richard Rovere, 'Eisenhower Over the Shoulder', *The American Scholar* XXI (Spring, 1962) pp. 34–44.

7. William L. O'Neill, *Coming Apart: An Informal History of America in the 1960s* (New York: Quadrangle, 1971) pp. 3–24.

8. Goldman, *The Crucial Decade*, p. 291.

9. O'Neill, *Coming Apart*, p. 4.

10. Godfrey Hodgson, *America in Our Time: From World War II to Nixon, What Happened and Why* (New York: Vintage Books, 1978) pp. 54–64.

11. Morris Dickstein, *Gates of Eden: American Culture in the Sixties* (New York: Basic Books, 1977) pp. 3–12.

12. Charlie Gillett, *The Sound of the City: The Rise of Rock and Roll* (New York: Bell, 1972).

13. Victor S. Navasky, *Naming Names* (New York: Viking, 1980).

14. Michel Ciment, *Kazan on Kazan* (New York: Viking, 1973).

15. Ibid., p. 94.

16. Peter Biskind and Dan Georgakas, 'An Exchange on Viva Zapata', *Cineaste* VII, 2 (Spring, 1976) pp. 10–17.

17. Ciment, *Kazan on Kazan*, p. 110.

18. Ibid., p. 108.

19. Nicholas Garnham, *Samuel Fuller* (New York: Viking, 1971).

20. Nora Sayre, *Running Time: Films of the Cold War* (New York: The Dial Press, 1982) p. 176.

21. Deborah Silverton Rosenfelt (ed.), *Salt of the Earth* (Old Westbury, New York: The Feminist Press, 1978).

22. Stuart Samuels, 'The Age of Conspiracy and Conformity: Invasion of the Body Snatchers', in John E. O'Connor and Martin A. Jackson (eds), *American History/American Film* (New York: Frederick Ungar, 1979) pp. 203–17.

23. Gordon Gow, *Hollywood in the Fifties* (New York: A. S. Barnes, 1971).

24. Michael Wood, *America in the Movies: Or, 'Santa Maria It Had Slipped My Mind!'* (New York: Basic Books, 1975) pp. 180–1.

25. Brandon French, *On the Verge of Revolt: Women in American Films of the Fifties* (New York: Frederick Ungar, 1978) pp. 2–12.

26. Robert Sklar, *Movie Made America: A Cultural History of American Movies* (New York: Vintage Books, 1975) pp. 283–4.

27. Wood, *America in the Movies*, pp. 146–64.

28. Ibid.

29. Phillip French, *Westerns* (New York: Oxford University Press, 1977) p. 70.

30. Ibid.

31. Molly Haskell, *From Reverence to Rape: The Treatment of Women in the Movies* (Baltimore, Maryland: Penguin, 1974) pp. 231–76.

32. Jon Halliday, *Sirk on Sirk* (New York: Viking, 1972) pp. 97–8.

33. Venable Herndon, *James Dean: A Short Life* (New York: Signet, 1974).

34. Garth Jowett, *Film: The Democratic Art* (Boston: Little, Brown and Company, 1976) p. 385.

35. Sidney Poitier, *This Life* (New York: Ballantine Books, 1980) pp. 331–41.

36. Eric Barnouw, *Tube of Plenty: The Evolution of American Television* (New York: Oxford University Press, 1977) pp. 154–65.

37. Norman Kagan, *The Cinema of Stanley Kubrick* (New York: Grove Press, 1972) pp. 47–67.

38. Donald Spoto, *Stanley Kramer: Filmmaker* (New York: G. P. Putnam's Sons, 1978) pp. 207–15.

4. THE SIXTIES

1. William L. Langer, *Political and Social Upheaval, 1832–1852* (New York: Harper and Row, 1969).

2. Godfrey Hodgson, *America in Our Time: From World War II to Nixon, What Happened and Why* (New York: Vintage, 1978).

3. Hodgson, *America in Our Time*, pp. 491–9.

4. William L. O'Neill, *Coming Apart: An informal History of America in the 1960s* (New York: Quadrangle, 1971) pp. 29–103.

5. Ibid.

6. Hodgson, *America in Our Time*, pp. 179–99.

7. Ibid.

8. Ibid.

9. Hodgson, *America in Our Time*, pp. 200–24.

10. Ibid.

11. Doris Kearns, *Lyndon B. Johnson and the American Dream* (New York: Signet, 1976) pp. 220–62.

12. Ibid., pp. 263–323.

13. Frances Fitzgerald, *Fire in the Lake* (New York: Vintage Books, 1973).

14. David Halberstam, *The Best and the Brightest* (New York: Fawcett, 1973).

15. Kirkpatrick Sale, *SDS* (New York: Vintage Books, 1974).

16. Morris Dickstein, *Gates of Eden: American Culture in the Sixties* (New York: Basic Books, 1977) pp. 51–88, 128–53.

17. Hodgson, *America in Our Time*, pp. 326–52.

18. O'Neill, *Coming Apart*, pp. 396–428.

19. Ibid.

20. James Monaco, *American Film Now: The People, The Power, The Money, The Movies* (New York: Oxford University Press, 1979) pp. 1–48.

21. Ibid.

22. Ibid.

23. Pauline Kael, *Going Steady* (New York: Bantam, 1971) p. 115.

24. Gerald Pratley, *The Cinema of John Frankenheimer* (Cranbury, New Jersey: A. S. Barnes, 1969).

25. Susan Sontag, *Against Interpretation* (New York: Dell, 1969) p. 215.

26. Norman Kagan, *The War Film* (New York: Pyramid Publications, 1974) p. 142.

27. Norman Kagan, *The Cinema of Stanley Kubrick* (New York: Grove Press, 1975) pp. 111–44.

28. Pauline Kael, *Kiss, Kiss, Bang, Bang* (New York: Bantam, 1969) p. 79.

29. Kagan, *The Cinema of Stanley Kubrick*, p. 132.

30. Donald Spoto, *Stanley Kramer: Filmmaker* (New York: G. P. Putnam's Sons, 1978) pp. 273–81.

31. Norman Mailer, *Armies of the Night* (New York: Signet, 1968) p. 47.

32. Robin Wood, *Arthur Penn* (New York: Praeger, 1969) pp. 72–91.

33. Hollis Alpert and Andrew Sarris (eds), *Film 68/69: An Anthology by the National Society of Film Critics* (New York: Simon and Schuster, 1969) pp. 235–41.

34. Alan G. Barbour, *John Wayne* (New York: Pyramid, 1974) pp. 121–2.

35. Renata Adler, *A Year in the Dark* (New York: Berkeley, 1969) pp. 199–200.

36. Joseph Morgenstern and Stefan Kanfer (eds), *Film 69/70: An Anthology by the National Society of Film Critics* (New York: Simon and Schuster, 1970) pp. 148–56.

37. Wood, *Arthur Penn*, pp. 92–116.

38. Morgenstern and Kanfer, *Film 69/70*, pp. 165–72.

39. Diana Trilling, *We Must March My Darlings* (New York: Harcourt Brace and Janovich, 1977) pp. 175–86.

5. THE SEVENTIES

1. Jonathan Schell, *The Time of Illusion* (New York: Alfred A. Knopf, 1976).

2. Godfrey Hodgson, *America in Our Time* (New York: Vintage Books, 1978) pp. 239–40.

3. Ibid., p. 398.

4. Schell, *The Time of Illusion*, pp. 77–134.

5. Theodore H. White, *Breach of Faith* (New York: Dell, 1975).

6. Gerald R. Ford, *A Time to Heal* (New York: Berkeley, 1980) pp. 378–80.

7. James Wooten, *Dasher* (New York: Signet, 1978).

8. Ibid., p. 298.

9. Ibid., p. 301.

10. Christopher Lasch, *The Culture of Narcissism* (New York: Warner Books, 1979).

11. Ibid.

12. Lou Cannon, *Ronald Reagan* (New York: G. P. Putnam's Sons, 1982).

13. James Monaco, *American Film Now* (New York: Oxford University Press, 1979) pp. 1–48.

14. Diane Jacobs, *Hollywood Renaissance: The New Generation of Filmmakers and Their Works* (New York: Delta, 1980).

15. Monaco, *American Film Now*, pp. 54–68.

16. Robert Warshow, *The Immediate Experience* (Garden City, New York: Anchor, 1964) p. 87.

17. Jacobs, *Hollywood Renaissance*, pp. 115–18.

18. Leonard Quart and Al Auster, 'The Godfather, Part II', *Cineaste*, vi, 4 (Winter, 1976) pp. 38–9.

19. Tom Wicker, quoted in Judith M. Kass, *Robert Altman: American Innovator* (New York: Popular Library, 1978) p. 193.

20. Leonard Quart, 'Altman's Films', *Marxist Perspectives*, i, i (Spring, 1978) pp. 21–33.

21. Molly Haskell, *From Reverence to Rape* (Baltimore, Maryland: Penguin Books, 1974) p. 366.

22. Ibid., p. 369.

23. Two of Scorsese's seventies' films, both starring Robert De Niro, were critical hits, the work of a genuine auteur: *Mean Streets* (1973), a tense jagged film fusing realistic and expressionist images to evoke the claustrophobic, violent world of a group of 'the boys' in New York's Little Italy; and *Taxi Driver* (1976) which focuses on the character of Travis Bickle, a lonely, frustrated and paranoid New York cab driver who is filled with terrifying rage. Though Bickle's rage centres on what he perceives as corrupt and decadent, the film is much more a reworking of forties' *film noir* conventions and an expression of Scorsese's and scriptwriter Paul Schrader's personal fantasies than a conscious critique of a corrupt 1970s America.

24. Leonard Quart and Barbara Quart, 'Kramer vs. Kramer', *Cineaste*, x, 2 (Spring, 1980) pp. 37–9.

25. Stuart M. Kaminsky, *Don Siegel, Director* (New York: Curtis Books, 1974) pp. 268–83.

26. Leonard Quart and Albert Auster, 'The Working Class Goes to Hollywood', in Philip Davies and Brian Neve (eds), *Cinema, Politics and Society in America* (Manchester: Manchester University Press, 1981) pp. 163–75.

27. Albert Auster and Leonard Quart, 'Saturday Night Fever', *Cineaste*, viii, 4 (Winter, 1978) pp. 36–7.

28. Peter Biskind, 'Jaws', *Jump Cut*, 15, pp. 3–4.

29. Dan Rubey, 'Star Wars', *Jump Cut*, 18, pp. 9–14.

30. Josh Rofkin, 'The Exorcist', *Screen Talk* (September, 1975) p. 54.

31. Albert Auster and Leonard Quart, 'Hollywood and Vietnam: The Triumph of the Will', *Cineaste*, ix, 3 (Spring, 1979) pp. 4–9.

32. Ibid.

33. Albert Auster and Leonard Quart, 'Man and Superman: Vietnam and the New American Hero', *Social Policy* (January–February, 1981) pp. 60–4.

6. THE EIGHTIES

1. Lou Cannon, *Ronald Reagan* (New York: G. P. Putnam's Sons, 1982) pp. 329–413.

2. Budd Schulberg, 'What Makes Hollywood Run Now?', *The New York Times*

Magazine (27 April 1980) pp. 52–88. See also Leslie Wayne, 'Hollywood Sequels Are Just the Ticket', *The New York Times* (18 July 1982) pp. 1, 17.

3. Veronica Geng, 'Pearls Before Swine. Review of Ordinary People', *Soho Weekly News* (17 September 1980) pp. 58–9.

4. Barbara Quart, 'Tootsie', *Cineaste*, XII, 4 (Summer, 1983) pp. 40–2.

5. Richard Schickel, 'Slam! Bang! A Movie Movie', *Time* (15 June 1981) pp. 74–6.

6. Michiko Kakutani, 'The Two Faces of Spielberg – Horror vs. Hope', *The New York Times* (30 May 1982) pp. 1, 30. See also Pauline Kael, 'The Pure and the Impure', *The New Yorker* (14 June 1982) pp. 119–22.

7. Richard Schickel, 'At Last, Kate and Hank!', *Time* (18 November 1981) pp. 112–13.

8. Aaron Latham, 'Warren Beatty, Seriously', *Rolling Stone* (1 April 1982) p. 19.

9. Belle Gale Chevigny, Kate Ellis, Ann Kaplan and Leonard Quart, 'Talking "Reds" ', *Socialist Review*, 12, 2 (March–April, 1982) pp. 109–24.

10. Ibid.

11. Robert A. Rosenstone, *Romantic Revolutionary: A Biography of John Reed* (New York: Alfred A. Knopf, 1975) p. 4.

12. Richard Grenier, 'Bolshevism for the 80's', *Commentary* (March, 1982) pp. 56–63.

13. Joy Gould Boyum, ' "Reds": Love and Revolution', *The Wall Street Journal* (4 December 1981) p. 35.

Bibliography

Dean Acheson, *Present at the Creation* (New York, 1969).

Renata G. Adler, *A Year in the Dark* (New York, 1969).

James Agee, *Agee on Film: Reviews and Comments* (Boston, 1966).

Hollis Alpert and Andrew Sarris (eds), *Film 68/69* (New York, 1969).

Rick Altman, *Genre: The Musical* (London, 1981).

Stephen Ambrose, *Rise to Globalism* (Baltimore, Md., 1971).

Alan G. Barbour, *John Wayne* (New York, 1974).

Eric Barnouw, *Tube of Plenty* (New York, 1977).

Donald Bogle, *Toms, Coons, Mulattoes, Mammies and Bucks* (New York, 1973).

Lou Cannon, *Ronald Reagan* (New York, 1982).

Frank Capra, *The Name Above the Title* (New York, 1972).

Michel Ciment, *Kazan on Kazan* (New York, 1973).

Alistair Cooke, *A Generation on Trial* (Baltimore, Md., 1952).

Philip Davies and Brian Neve (eds), *Cinema, Politics and Society in America* (Manchester, 1981).

Barbara Deming, *Running Away From Myself* (New York, 1969).

Morris Dickstein, *Gates of Eden* (New York, 1977).

Frances Fitzgerald, *Fire in the Lake* (New York, 1973).

Gerald R. Ford, *A Time to Heal* (New York, 1980).

Hugh Fordin, *The World of Entertainment. Hollywood's Greatest Musicals* (Garden City, New York, 1975).

Brandon French, *On the Verge of Revolt: Women in American Films of the Fifties* (New York, 1978).

Phillip French, *Westerns* (New York, 1977).

Nicholas Garnham, *Samuel Fuller* (New York, 1971).

Charlie Gillett, *The Sound of the City: The Rise and Fall of Rock and Roll* (New York, 1972).

Eric Goldman, *The Crucial Decade – and After, America 1945–1960* (New York, 1960).

Walter Goodman, *The Committee* (Baltimore, Md., 1969).

Joseph G. Goulden, *The Best Years, 1945–1950* (New York, 1976).

Gordon Gow, *Hollywood in the Fifties* (New York, 1971).

David Halberstam, *The Best and the Brightest* (New York, 1973).

Stuart Hall and Paddy Whannel, *The Popular Arts* (New York, 1965).

Jon Halliday, *Sirk on Sirk* (New York, 1972).

Molly Haskell, *From Reverence to Rape* (Baltimore, Md., 1974).

Venable Herndon, *James Dean: A Short Life* (New York, 1974).

Charles Higham and Joel Greenberg, *Hollywood in the Forties* (New York, 1970).

Godfrey Hodgson, *America in Our Time* (New York, 1978).

Diane Jacobs, *Hollywood Renaissance* (New York, 1981).

Pauline Kael, *Kiss, Kiss, Bang, Bang* (New York, 1969).

Pauline Kael, *Going Steady* (New York, 1971).

Norman Kagan, *The Cinema of Stanley Kubrick* (New York, 1972).

Norman Kagan, *The War Film* (New York, 1974).

Stuart M. Kaminsky, *Don Siegel, Director* (New York, 1974).

Judith Kass, *Robert Altman: American Innovator* (New York, 1978).

Doris Kearns, *Lyndon B. Johnson and the American Dream* (New York, 1976).

Siegfried Kracauer, *From Caligari to Hitler*, 3rd ed. (Princeton, New Jersey, 1970).

William L. Langer, *Political and Social Upheaval, 1832–1852* (New York, 1969).

Christopher Lasch, *The Culture of Narcissism* (New York, 1979).

Norman Mailer, *Armies of the Night* (New York, 1968).

Gerald Mast and Marshall Cohen (eds), *Film Theory and Criticism* (New York, 1979).

James Monaco, *American Film Now* (New York, 1979).

Joseph Morgenstern and Stefan Kanfer (eds), *Film 69/70* (New York, 1970).

Victor S. Navasky, *Naming Names* (New York, 1980).

John E. O'Connor and Martin A. Jackson, *American History/American Film: Interpreting the Hollywood Image* (New York, 1979).

William L. O'Neill, *Coming Apart: An Informal History of America in the 1960s* (New York, 1971).

Sidney Poitier, *This Life* (New York, 1980).

Gerald Pratley, *The Cinema of John Frankenheimer* (Cranbury, New Jersey, 1969).

Peter Roffman and Jim Purdy, *The Hollywood Social Problem Film* (Bloomington, Indiana, 1981).

Deborah Silverton Rosenfelt (ed.), *Salt of the Earth* (Old Westbury, New York, 1976).

Robert Rosenstone, *Romantic Revolutionary: A Biography of John Reed* (New York, 1975).

Richard Rovere, *Senator Joseph McCarthy* (New York, 1971).

Kirkpatrick Sale, *SDS* (New York, 1974).

Nora Sayre, *Running Time* (New York, 1982).

Jonathan Schell, *The Time of Illusion* (New York, 1976).

Robert Sklar, *Movie Made America* (New York, 1975).

Susan Sontag, *Against Interpretation* (New York, 1969).

Donald Spoto, *Stanley Kramer; Filmmaker* (New York, 1978).

Diana Trilling, *We Must March My Darlings* (New York, 1977).

Robert Warshow, *The Immediate Experience* (Garden City, New York, 1964).

Theodore H. White, *Breach of Faith* (New York, 1980).

Raymond Williams, *Communications* (London, 1976).

Michael Wood, *America in the Movies* (New York, 1975).

Robin Wood, *Arthur Penn* (New York, 1969).

James Wooten, *Dasher* (New York, 1978).

Index

Directors are shown for films only when they are named in the text.